# Talking Anarchy

# Talking Anarchy

Colin Ward
&
David Goodway

PMPRESS

*Talking Anarchy*
Colin Ward and David Goodway

First published 2003 by Five Leaves Publications
This edition © PM Press 2014

PO Box 23912
Oakland, CA 94623
www.pmpress.org

Cover design by John Yates
Layout by Jonathan Rowland

This book has been made possible in part by a generous donation
from the Anarchist Archives Project.

ISBN: 978-1-60486-812-8
LCCN: 2013911527

10 9 8 7 6 5 4 3 2 1

Printed in the USA, by the Employee Owners of Thomson-Shore in
Dexter, Michigan.
www.thomsonshore.com

# Contents

# PREFACE

The origins of this book and the way it was compiled are curious and likely to interest its readers, old and new. In April 2001 Colin Ward acceded to the badgering over many years of his friends Amedeo Bertolo and Rossella Di Leo, finally agreeing to be included in the series of book-length interviews their impressive imprint Elèuthera was publishing in Milan and to take his place alongside such luminaries of radical culture as Ivan Illich, Paulo Freire, Giancarlo De Carlo, Judith Malina, Enrico Baj, and Evelyn Fox Keller. The format was that the interviewer wrote a substantial introduction about the subject and appeared as the sole of author of the book. Colin asked me to fulfil this role for *Conversazioni con Colin Ward*, but I didn't want to, being committed to other projects. He persisted saying it would involve me in little or no work! He explained that my essay "The Anarchism of Colin Ward," which I'd written for his *festschrift*, *Richer Futures: Fashioning a New Politics* (edited by Ken Worpole in 1999), could be reprinted unchanged as the introduction. This was definitely encouraging since it implied he approved of its content. Further—and this was really surprising—I wouldn't need to travel from Yorkshire in the North of England to interview him at his home in East Anglia, because our discussions could be carried out just as well by letter.

And so we began work on the book. I started, I see, by sending him twenty-seven groups of questions, asking him in part about the kind of anarchist he was and his early years and his participation in the Freedom Press Group. The result was the nearest he ever came to autobiography and is the section of *Talking Anarchy* I consider especially valuable. After this I provided more questions, but just as often he would send answers to questions he had written himself and was also "answering." Perhaps he had originally believed the entire interview section could be constructed in this way, but I hung on in terrier fashion, insisting on a significant input if my name was to appear as the interviewer. At the outset he had worked out the minimum length acceptable in Milan: "You will see that the Di Carlo book is long and the Freire one short (and in a larger typeface) so they are obviously flexible about length" (2 May 2001). When we, particularly he, seemed to have exhausted the obvious topics, we had to work hard to make up the shortfall of words, turning to the section on current events which concludes the book, a real dialogue developing for the first time. Throughout he would type both questions and answers and retype as necessary, cutting and pasting in the old physical sense, with many trips to the photocopier in a local shop. (He was never to word-process or use a computer.)

Our agreed typescript was then dispatched to Amedeo and Rossella, who had a translator on hand to produce the Italian version. Throughout the process, though, I had worked hard to ensure we had a good text since my assumption was that publication in English would follow hard upon the appearance of *Conversazioni con Colin Ward*. I told Ross Bradshaw, who was reprinting several of Colin's works as well as commissioning a new one, about *Conversazioni* and sent the manuscript, which he read excitedly and said he definitely wanted to publish as a Five Leaves title even before he had fully read it. Colin's reaction was perplexing: he would not countenance an English edition in his lifetime. Colin was by then seventy-nine and tried to allay my disappointment, several times, telling me to "remember that it won't be all that long when you have to introduce an English version for Ross Bradshaw!" (15 March 2003). Yet Ross's response was that he was only interested in bringing the book out while Colin was still alive.

There matters rested for several months. Then, entirely unexpectedly, Colin telephoned to say he was allowing Five Leaves to publish. Why the change of mind? He had just been interviewed by a young researcher and had had some difficulty in recalling things (although in my own experience his long-term memory continued to be as meticulously detailed as ever); and I believe he felt that what Ross was to title *Talking Anarchy* would be a useful tool to fob off future interviewers.

Ross maintained his enthusiasm for the book, merely criticizing its "blandness," commenting on the number of times Colin and I had said "I agree." I told Ross I entirely concurred, but that my attempts to stir Colin up and to introduce a little controversy had been overruled and eliminated. An indication of his benign temperament comes (on p. 45) when he mentioned the "networks of anarchists in a city the size of London who could engage in, or stay aloof from, the activities of Freedom Press." I responded eagerly: "That's an interesting remark! Who stayed aloof?" and he retorted: "I think it is inevitable rather than interesting." I realized he felt uncomfortable with Murray Bookchin and his style of anarchism and quoted what Murray (equally uncomprehending in reverse) had recently jested to me: "If an additional traffic light were installed in Trafalgar

Square Colin would consider the Revolution had come."
The most I was allowed appears on p. 111:

> Colin, you are such a generous person, always un-
> willing to be critical of fellow anarchists. Yet you
> imply that there are "things" which "divide" you
> from Murray. Is it simply a matter of high theory,
> of style and changing opinions, all of which you
> have touched upon, or do you consider more fun-
> damental issues separate your respective, very dis-
> tinctive conceptions of anarchism?

To which he countered:

> It isn't that I am kind or generous. It is simply that
> I take seriously the business of being an anarchist
> propagandist. Nothing makes us more ridiculous
> in the eyes of the world outside than the internal
> factional disputes some anarchists enjoy pursuing.
> I try to avoid them.

(For the record, I would observe that I also continue to
admire Murray Bookchin greatly.)

Working with Colin on what became *Talking Anarchy*
was an intense but delightful experience. Zach Blue of AK
Press was to comment on what a pleasure it must have
been to have interviewed him. I broke to it to Zach that we
had never met during the process, but was much relieved
that the text apparently reads like a genuine interview. It
seems easily the work of mine most appreciated by readers. That is of course because it is essentially a book by the
great, good and unfailingly lovable Colin Ward.

David Goodway

# INTRODUCTION

Colin Ward is one of the great radical figures of the past half-century, but his impact has been subterranean. His name is little mentioned by commentators and is scarcely known to the wider, intelligent public, even in his native Britain. A striking indication of his intellectual and institutional marginality is that he did not even possess a regular commercial publisher. In *Richer Futures: Fashioning a New Politics* (1999), a *festschrift* intended at least in part to remedy this unsatisfactory state of affairs, the editor, Ken Worpole, ably demonstrated the correspondence between Ward's concerns and contemporary debates and problems. I suspect that Ward himself would have contended that this linkage can be made because of the commonsensical, realistic, *necessary* nature of anarchism as such (and not just his especial brand), if people could only see that, and its obvious relevance to the needs of the 21st century; and with this I myself would agree to a considerable extent. But equally there can be no gainsaying the very real originality of his oeuvre.

Colin Ward was born on 14 August 1924 in Wanstead, in suburban Essex, the son of Arnold Ward, a teacher, and Ruby Ward (née West), who had been a shorthand typist. He was educated at the County High School for Boys, Ilford (whose other principal claim to fame is that for thirty-eight years its English teacher was the father of the well-known poet and critic, Kathleen Raine, who was to write venomously and extremely snobbishly of him, the school, and Ilford in her first volume of autobiography, *Farewell Happy Fields*). Ward was an unsuccessful pupil and left school at fifteen.

Arnold Ward taught in elementary schools, eventually becoming a headmaster, in West Ham which, although a county borough outside the London County Council, contained the depths of poverty of Canning Town and Silvertown. He was a natural Labour supporter and the family car was much in demand on polling days. To grow up in a strongly Labour Party environment in the 1930s was far from stultifying as is attested by Colin Ward having both heard Emma Goldman speak in 1938, at the massive May Day rally in Hyde Park, and attended in April 1939 the "Festival of Music for the People" at which Benjamin Britten's *Ballad of Heroes*, with a libretto by W.H. Auden and Randall Swingler, and conducted by Constant Lambert, saluted the fallen of the International Brigades at the Queen's Hall. He also recalls the milk tokens, a voluntary surcharge on milk sales, by which the London Co-operative Society raised a levy for Spanish relief.

It was Ward's experiences during the Second World War that shaped, to a very large extent, his later career. His first job was as a clerk for a builder erecting (entirely fraudulently) air-raid shelters. His next was in the Ilford Borough Engineer's office, where his eyes were opened to the inequitable treatment of council-house tenants, with some having requests for repairs attended to immediately, while others had to wait since they ranked low in an unspoken hierarchy of estates. He then went to work for the architect Sidney Caulfield, a living link with the Arts and Crafts Movement since he had been articled to John Loughborough Pearson (for whom he had worked on Truro Cathedral), been taught lettering by Edward Johnson and Eric Gill, and also, at the Central School of Arts and Crafts, studied under and later worked as a colleague of W.R. Lethaby, whom Caulfield revered. Lethaby, a major architectural thinker as well as architect, is one of the nine people whom Ward was to name in 1991 in his *Influences*. Next door to his office, Caulfield—who was brother-in-law to Britain's solitary Futurist painter, C.R.W. Nevinson—let a flat at 28 Emperor's Gate to Miron Grindea, the Romanian editor of the long-running little magazine, *Adam*. It was Grindea who introduced Ward to the work of such writers as Proust, Gide, Thomas Mann, Brecht, Lorca, and Canetti.

On demobilisation from the British Army in 1947 Ward went back to work for Caulfield for eighteen months, before moving to the Architects' Co-partnership (which had been formed before the war as the Architects' Co-operative Partnership by a group of Communists who had been students together at the Architectural Association School). From 1952 to 1961 he was a senior assistant to Shepheard & Epstein, whose practice was devoted entirely to schools and municipal housing, and then worked for two years as director of research for Chamberlin, Powell, and Bon. After a career change to teaching in 1964—he was in charge of liberal studies at Wandsworth Technical College from 1966—he returned to architecture and planning in 1971 by becoming education officer for the Town and Country Planning Association (founded by Ebenezer Howard as the Garden City Association) for which he edited *BEE* (*Bulletin of Environmental Education*). He resigned in 1979, moved to the Suffolk countryside, and became a self-employed author.

Ward had been conscripted in 1942 and it was then that he came into contact with anarchists. Posted to

Glasgow, he received "a real education" there: on account of the eye-catching deprivation, his use of the excellent Mitchell Library and, as the only British city ever to have had a significant indigenous anarchist movement (in contrast to London's Continental exiles and Jewish immigrants), the dazzling anarchist orators on Glasgow Green with their Sunday-night meetings in a room above the Hangman's Rest in Wilson Street and bookshop in George Street.[1] He was particularly influenced by Frank Leech, a shopkeeper and former miner, who urged him to submit articles to *War Commentary* in London—the first, "Allied Military Government," on the new order in liberated Europe, appeared in December 1943. After visiting Leech, sentenced for failing to register for fire-watching and refusing to pay the fine, while on hunger strike in Barlinnie Prison, Ward, who had no clothes to wear other than his uniform, found himself transferred to Orkney and Shetland for the remainder of the war.

It was in April 1945, as the war drew to a close, that the four editors of *War Commentary* were prosecuted for conspiring to cause disaffection in the armed forces—they were anticipating a revolutionary situation comparable to that in Russia and Germany at the end of the First World War, one of their headlines insisting "Hang on to Your Arms!"—and Ward was among four servicemen subscribers who were called to give evidence for the prosecution. All four testified that they had not been disaffected; but John Hewetson, Vernon (Vero) Richards, and Philip Sansom were each imprisoned for nine months (Marie Louise Berneri was acquitted on the technicality that she was married to Richards). The following year, still in the army, but now in the South of England, Ward was able

---

1   All otherwise unacknowledged quotations derive from an interview with Colin Ward of 29 June 1997.

to report on the postwar squatters' movement in nine articles in *Freedom* (*War Commentary* having reverted to its traditional title); and when he was eventually discharged from the army in the summer of 1947, he was asked to join *Freedom*'s editorial group, of which George Woodcock had also been a member since 1945. This was his first close contact with the people who were to become his "closest and dearest friends."

This Freedom Press Group was extremely talented and energetic and, although Woodcock emigrated to Canada in 1949 and Berneri died the same year, was able to call upon contributions from anarchists like Herbert Read (until ostracized in 1953 for accepting a knighthood), Alex Comfort and the political scientist Geoffrey Ostergaard and such sympathisers as Gerald Brenan.[2] The file of *Freedom* for the late 1940s and early 1950s makes impressive reading. During the 1940s *War Commentary*, followed by *Freedom*, had been fortnightly, but from summer 1951 the paper went weekly. The bulk of the contents had always been written by the editors; and in 1950 Ward had provided some twenty-five items, rising to no fewer than fifty-four in 1951, but the number declined as he began to contribute long articles, frequently spread over four to six issues. From May 1956 until the end of 1960, and now using the heading of "People and Ideas," he wrote around 165 such columns. Given this daunting, spare-time journalistic apprenticeship, it is hardly surprising that his stylistic vice

---

2    Geoffrey Ostergaard (1926–90), who spent his entire career at the University of Birmingham, wrote on three areas: syndicalism and workers' control (for *Freedom* and *Anarchy*), the British co-operative movement, and the Sarvodaya movement of India. Gerald Brenan (1894–1987), a member of the Bloomsbury Group, lived for most of his long life in Spain, becoming a notable Hispanicist and author of a major work of history, *The Spanish Labyrinth* (1943), his exploration of the origins of the Civil War.

continued to be the excessive employment of lengthy, partially digested quotations.

By the early 1950s characteristic Ward topics had emerged: housing and planning, workers' control and self-organization in industry, the problems of making rural life economically viable, the decolonizing societies. He was alert to what was going on in the wider intellectual world, attempting to point to what was happening outside the confines of anarchism, drawing on the developing sociological literature, and, for example, writing (sympathetically) on Bertolt Brecht (5 August and 1 September 1956) and excitedly highlighting the publication in *Encounter* of Isaiah Berlin's Third Programme talks on BBC radio on the Russian intelligentsia between 1838 and 1848, "A Marvellous Decade," and much later to be collected in *Russian Thinkers* (25 June 1955). But who was reading his articles? *War Commentary* had fared relatively well in wartime on account of the solidarity and intercourse between the small anti-war groups, principally *Peace News*, but also the ILP (Independent Labour Party) with its *New Leader*. With the end of the war and Labour's electoral triumph in 1945, the anarchists were to become very isolated indeed—Freedom Press was unswervingly hostile to the Labour governments and their welfare legislation. Ward recalls Marie Louise Berneri saying towards the end of the forties: "The paper gets better and better, and fewer and fewer people read it." The isolation and numerical insignificance of British anarchism obtained throughout the fifties also.

It was to break from the treadmill of weekly production that Ward began to urge the case for a monthly, more reflective *Freedom*; and eventually his fellow editors responded by giving him his head with the monthly *Anarchy* from March 1961, while they continued to bring out *Freedom* for the other three weeks of each month. Ward had actually wanted the monthly to be called *Autonomy: A Journal of Anarchist Ideas*, but this his traditionalist comrades were not prepared to allow (he had already been described as a "revisionist"[3] and they considered that he was backing away from the talismanic word "anarchist"), although the subtitle was initially, and now largely redundantly, retained. One hundred eighteen issues were to appear, culminating in December 1970, with a series of superb covers designed by Rufus Segar.

In a review of the 1950s and statement of his personal agenda for the 1960s Ward had observed:

> The anarchist movement throughout the world can hardly be said to have increased its influence during the decade . . . Yet the relevance of anarchist ideas was never so great. Anarchism suffers, as all minority movements suffer, from the fact that its numerical weakness inhibits its intellectual strength. This may not matter when you approach it as individual attitude to life, but in its other role, as a social theory, as one of the possible approaches to the solution of the problems of social life, it is a very serious thing. It is precisely this lack which people have in mind when they complain that there have been no advances in anarchist theory since the days of Kropotkin. Ideas and not armies change the face of the world, and in the sphere of what we ambitiously call the social sciences, too few of the people with ideas couple them with anarchist attitudes.
>
> For the anarchists the problem of the nineteen-sixties is simply that of how to put anarchism back

---

3    Colin Ward, "Notes of an Anarchist Columnist," *The Raven,* no. 12 (October/December 1990), p. 316.

into the intellectual bloodstream, into the field of
ideas which are taken seriously.[4]

As editor of *Anarchy* Ward had some success in putting
anarchist ideas "back into the intellectual bloodstream,"
largely because of propitious political and social changes.
The rise of the New Left and the nuclear disarmament
movement in the late fifties, culminating in the student
radicalism and general libertarianism of the sixties,
meant that a new audience receptive to anarchist attitudes came into existence. My own case provides an illustration of the trend. In October 1961, a foundation sub-
scriber to the *New Left Review* (the first number of which
had appeared at the beginning of the previous year) and
in London again to appear at Bow Street after my arrest
during the Committee of 100 sit-down of 17 September,
I bought a copy of *Anarchy 8* in the Charing Cross Road
at Collets. I had just turned nineteen and thereafter was
hooked. When I went up to Oxford University twelve
months later I co-founded the Oxford Anarchist Group
and one of the first speakers I invited was Colin Ward (he
spoke on "Anarchism and the Welfare State" on 28 October
1963). Among the members were Gene Sharp, Richard
Mabey, Hugh Brody, Kate Soper, and Carole Pateman.[5]

---

4    "Last Look Round at the 50s," *Freedom*, 26 December 1959.
5    Gene Sharp was different from the rest of us since he was
American, much older (born 1928) and a postgraduate student,
who had already published extensively on non-violent direct action—as he has continued to do, *The Politics of Nonviolent Action*
(1973) being especially noteworthy. Richard Mabey, after working
in publishing where he edited several of Colin Ward's books, went
on to become a successful writer on botany and wildlife, initially
with a markedly alternative approach: for example, *Food for Free*
and *The Unofficial Countryside*. Hugh Brody is many things, but
principally an anthropologist, authority on the Canadian Inuit
and advocate of the way of life of hunter-gatherers, as in the

The Marxist social historian, Raphael Samuel, was later to tell me that he had attended some of our meetings. By 1968 Ward himself could say in a radio interview: "I think that social attitudes have changed . . . Anarchism perhaps is becoming almost modish. I think that there is a certain anarchy in the air today . . ."[6]

Ward's success was also due to *Anarchy*'s simple excellence. This should not be exaggerated, for there was definite unevenness. The editing, according to an admiring, though not uncritical contributor (Nicolas Walter), was minimal: nothing was re-written, nothing even subbed. "Colin almost didn't do anything. He didn't muck it about, didn't really bother to read the proofs. Just shoved them all in. Just let it happen."[7] Ward put the contents together on his kitchen table. Coming out of *Freedom*, he frequently wrote much of the journal himself under a string of pseudonyms—John Ellerby, John Schubert (these two after the streets where he was currently living), Tristram Shandy—as well as the unsigned items. Even the articles scarcely differed from, and indeed there was significant recycling of, his contributions to *Freedom* back in the 1950s—for example, the admired issue on adventure playgrounds

---

acclaimed *The Other Side of Eden* being his latest book. Kate Soper became a Marxist philosopher, author of *On Human Needs* and member of the editorial committee of the *New Left Review*, but is also one of the translators of Cornelius Castoriadis into English. Carole Pateman, then an assistant in the original Oxfam shop, is now a distinguished libertarian and feminist political philosopher—her works include *The Problem of Political Obligation*, *The Sexual Contract*, and *The Disorder of Women*—and a Professor at the University of California, Los Angeles.

6    Richard Boston, "Conversations about Anarchism," *Anarchy*, no. 85 (March 1968), p. 74.

7    Quoted by Raphael Samuel, in an exceptionally generous evaluation, occasioned by the publication of *A Decade of Anarchy*, in *New Society*, 2 October 1987.

(September 1961) had been preceded by a similar piece in *Freedom* (6 September 1958). Sales never exceeded 2,800 per issue, no advance on *Freedom*'s 2,000 to 3,000.

The excellence, though, lay in a variety of factors. Ward's anarchism was no longer buried among reports of industrial disputes and comment on contemporary politics, whether national or international. It now stood by itself, supported by like-minded contributors. *Anarchy* exuded vitality, was in touch with the trends of its decade, and appealed to the young. Its preoccupations centred on housing and squatting, progressive education, workers' control (a theme shared with the New Left), and crime and punishment. The leading members of "the New Criminology"—David Downes, Jock Young (who had been a student distributor of *Anarchy* at the London School of Economics), Laurie Taylor, Stan Cohen, and Ian Taylor—all appeared in its pages. From the other side of the Atlantic the powerfully original essays by Murray Bookchin (initially as "Lewis Herber")—"Ecology and Revolutionary Thought" (November 1966), "Towards a Liberatory Technology" (August 1967), and "Desire and Need" (October 1967)—later collected in *Post-Scarcity Anarchism* (London, 1974)—had their first European publication in *Anarchy*.

It was his editorship of *Anarchy* that released Ward from the obscurity of *Freedom* and Freedom Press and made his name. During the 1960s he began to be asked to write for other journals, not only in the realm of dissident politics, like *Peace News* and *Liberation* (New York), but such titles as *The Twentieth Century* and the recently established *New Society*. Paul Barker was to invite him in 1978 to become a regular contributor to *New Society*'s full-page "Stand" column; and when *New Society* was merged with the *New Statesman* in 1988 he was retained as a columnist of the resultant *New Statesman and Society* with the shorter, but weekly, "Fringe Benefits," until its abrupt termination by a new editor in 1996. His first books, *Violence* and *Work*, came as late as 1970 and 1972 respectively, but these were intended for teenagers and published by Penguin Education in a series edited by Richard Mabey.

Ward's third book, which appeared in 1973, was his first for an adult readership and his only work on the theory of anarchism, indeed the only one "directly and specifically about anarchism" until the publication of *Anarchism: A Very Short Introduction*, which happened to be his final book.[8] It is also the one that has been most translated, currently into seven or possibly eight languages, for it is, as George Woodcock considered, "one of the most important theoretical works" on anarchism.[9] Ward had wanted to call it *Anarchy as a Theory of Organisation*—the title of an article that had appeared in *Anarchy* 62 (April 1966)—but the publishers, Allen & Unwin, insisted on *Anarchy in Action*.

It is in *Anarchy in Action* that Ward makes entirely explicit the highly distinctive anarchism that had informed his editorship of and contributions to *Anarchy* during the preceding decade. His opening words—alluding to Ignazio Silone's marvellous novel, *The Seed beneath the Snow* (1943), which he remembers reading on the train back to Orkney after a leave in London—have been much quoted:

> The argument of this book is that an anarchist society, a society which organises itself without authority, is always in existence, like a seed beneath

---

8    Colin Ward, "'I think that's a terrible thing to say!' Elderly anarchist hack tells all," in *Freedom: A Hundred Years* (*Freedom* Centenary Edition, October 1986), p. 63.

9    George Woodcock, *Anarchism and Anarchists: Essays* (Kingston, Ontario: Quarry Press, 1992), p. 231.

> the snow, buried under the weight of the state and
> its bureaucracy, capitalism and its waste, privilege
> and its injustices, nationalism and its suicidal loy-
> alties, religious differences and their superstitious
> separatism.

His kind of anarchism, "far from being a speculative vision of a future society . . . is a description of a mode of
human organisation, rooted in the experience of everyday
life, which operates side by side with, and in spite of, the
dominant authoritarian trends of our society."[10]

Acceptance of this central insight is not only extraor-
dinarily liberating intellectually but has strictly realistic
and practical consequences: ". . . once you begin to look at
human society from an anarchist point of view you discover
that the alternatives are already there, in the interstices of
the dominant power structure. If you want to build a free
society, the parts are all at hand."[11] It also solves two apparently insoluble problems that have always confronted
anarchists (and socialists). The first is, if anarchism (or socialism) is so highly desirable as well as feasible, how is it
that it has never come into being or lasted no longer than
a few months (or years). Ward's answer is that anarchism
is already partially in existence and that he can show us
examples "in action." The second problem is how can humans be taught to become cooperative, thereby enabling
a transition from the present order to a co-operative society to be attained. Ward's response here is that humans
are naturally co-operative and that current societies and
institutions, however capitalist and individualist, would
completely fall apart without the integrating powers, even

10   Colin Ward, *Anarchy in Action* (London: Allen & Unwin,
1973), p. 11.
11   *Ibid*, p. 13.

if unvalued, of mutual aid and federation. Nor will social transformation be a matter of climactic revolution, attained in a millennial moment, but rather a prolonged situation of dual power in the age-old struggle between authoritarian and libertarian tendencies, with outright victory for either tendency most improbable.

According to this conception of anarchism, as George Woodcock observes:

> . . . the anarchist seeks . . . not to destroy the present political order so that it may be replaced by a better system of organising . . . Rather, anarchism proposes to clear the existing structure of coercive institutions so that the natural society which has survived in a largely subterranean way from earlier, freer, and more originative periods can be liberated to flower again in a different future. The anarchists have never been nihilists, wishing to destroy present society entirely and replace it by something new . . . The anarchists have always valued the endurance of natural social impulses and the voluntary institutions they create, and it is to liberating the great network of human co-operation that even now spreads through all levels of our lives rather than to creating or even imagining brave new world[s] that they have bent their efforts. That is why there are so few utopian writings among the anarchists; they have always believed that human social instincts, once set free, could be trusted to adapt society in desirable and practical ways without plans—which are always [constrictive]—being made beforehand.[12]

---

12   Woodcock, *Anarchism and Anarchists*, p. 231.

Anarchists seek, in summary form, the end (that is, the goal) of voluntary co-operation or mutual aid by using the means of direct action, while organising freely. Ward is primarily concerned with the forms of direct action, in the world of the here-and-now, which are "liberating the great network of human co-operation." Back in 1973 he considered that "the very growth of the state and its bureaucracy, the giant corporation and its privileged hierarchy . . . are . . . giving rise to parallel organisations, counter organisations, alternative organisations, which exemplify the anarchist method"; and he proceeded to itemise the revived demand for workers' control, the de-schooling movement, self-help therapeutic groups, squatter movements and tenants' co-operatives, food co-operatives, claimants' unions, and community organisations of every conceivable kind.[13] During the following thirty years he additionally drew attention to self-build activities (he was been particularly impressed by achievements in the shanty towns in the poor countries of Latin America, Africa, and Asia), co-operatives of all types, the informal economy, and LETS (Local Exchange Trading Schemes). New self-organizing activities are continually emerging; "'Do-it-yourself' is . . . the essence of anarchist action, and the more people apply it on every level, in education, in the workplace, in the family, the more ineffective restrictive structures will become and the more dependence will be replaced by individual and collective self-reliance." This is another quotation from Woodcock, who was one of the most appreciative and perceptive of Ward's commentators; but otherwise discussion of his writings has been remarkably limited, presumably because they are perceived as insufficiently theoretical.[14]

---

13  Ward, *Anarchy in Action*, p. 137.
14  George Woodcock, *Anarchism: A History of Libertarian Ideas*

It is Ward's vision of anarchism, along with his many years of working in architecture and planning, that account for his concentration on "anarchist applications" or "anarchist solutions" to "immediate issues in which people *are actually likely to get involved* . . ."[15] Although he told me in 1997 that in his opinion "all my books hang together as an exploration of the relations between people and their environment" (by which he means the built, rather than the "natural," environment), and while this clearly covers nine-tenths of his output, it seems rather (as he had put it thirteen years earlier) that all his publications are "looking at life from an anarchist point of view."[16] So the "anarchist applications" concern housing: *Tenants Take Over* (1974), *Housing: An Anarchist Approach* (1976), *When We Build Again, Let's Have Housing That Works!* (1985), *Talking Houses* (1990), and *Cotters and Squatters* (2002); architecture and planning: *Welcome, Thinner City* (1989), *New Town, Home Town* (1993), *Talking to Architects* (1996), and *Sociable Cities* (with Peter Hall) (1998); education: *Talking Schools* (1995); education and the environment: *Streetwork: The Exploding School* (with Anthony Fyson) (1973), *The Child in the City* (1978) and *The Child in the Country* (1988); education, work, and housing: *Havens and Springboards* (1997); education and housing: *Undermining the Central Line* (with Ruth Rendell) (1989); transport: *Freedom to Go* (1991); and water: *Reflected in Water* (1997).

How did Ward come to espouse such an anarchism? Who are the thinkers and which are the traditions

---

*and Movements* (Harmondsworth: Penguin Books, 2nd edn., 1986), p. 421.

15   David Goodway (ed.), *For Anarchism: History, Theory, and Practice* (London: Routledge, 1989), p. 14; Colin Ward (ed.), *A Decade of Anarchy, 1961–1970: Selections from the Monthly Journal 'Anarchy'* (London: Freedom Press, 1987), p. 279.

16   Goodway, p. 21 n52.

responsible for shaping his outlook? First, it should be said that some would argue that there is no original- ity in Wardian anarchism since it is all anticipated by Peter Kropotkin and Gustav Landauer. There is indeed no denying Ward's very considerable debt to Kropotkin. He named Kropotkin as his economic influence; described himself as "an anarchist-communist, in the Kropotkin tra- dition"; and, regarding *Fields, Factories and Workshops* as "one of those great prophetic works of the nineteenth century whose hour is yet to come," brought it up to date as *Fields, Factories and Workshops Tomorrow* (1974).[17] It is also the case that Kropotkin in his great *Mutual Aid* demonstrates that co-operation is pervasive within both the animal and the human worlds, in his concluding chapter giving contemporary clubs and voluntary societ- ies, such as the Lifeboat Association, as examples. Ward, with his typical modesty, writes that in a sense *Anarchy in Action* is "simply an extended, updating footnote to Kropotkin's *Mutual Aid*."[18] Yet Kropotkin prepared for a bloody social revolution; and Ward also goes far beyond him in the types of co-operative groups he identifies in modern societies and the centrality he accords to them in anarchist transformation.

Ward is still closer to the remarkable Landauer. He even goes so far as to say that his "is not a new version of anarchism. Gustav Landauer saw it, not as the found- ing of something new, 'but as the actualisation and re- constitution of something that has always been present, which exists alongside the state, albeit buried and laid waste.'" One of Ward's favourite quotations, which he

---

17    Boston, p. 65; Peter Kropotkin, *Fields, Factories and Workshops Today* (London: Freedom Press, 2nd edn., 1985), p. iv.
18    Colin Ward, *Anarchy in Action* (London: Freedom Press, 2nd edn., 1996), p. 8.

rightly regarded as "a profound and simple contribution to the analysis of the state and society in one sentence" derives from an article by Landauer of 1910: "The state is not something which can be destroyed by a revolution, but is a condition, a certain relationship between human beings, a mode of human behaviour; we destroy it by contracting other relationships, by behaving differently."[19] What this led Landauer to advocate was the formation of producers' and consumers' co-operatives, but especially of agrarian communes; and his emphasis is substantially different to Ward's exploration of "anarchist solutions" to "immediate issues." In any case, for many years Ward only knew of Landauer through a chapter in Martin Buber's *Paths in Utopia* (1949); and it was Buber, who had been Landauer's friend and editor and shared similar views concerning the relationship between society and the state but, although sympathetic, was not an anarchist himself, whom Ward acknowledged as his influence with respect to "society." It seems extraordinary that Wardian anarchism was nurtured within a Freedom Press Group whose other members were looking back to the workers' and soldiers' councils of the Russian and German Revolutions and the collectives of the Spanish Revolution. He never believed in an imminent revolution: "That's just not my view of anarchism. I think it's unhistorical . . . I don't think you'll ever see any of my writings in *Freedom* which are remotely demanding revolution next week." When he tried to interest his comrades in the late 1940s in a pamphlet on the squatters' movement—to give them the idea he had even pasted his articles up—he recalls that "it wasn't thought that this is somehow relevant to anarchism." Although they deserve great credit for allowing him to go his own way

---

19   Ward, *Anarchy in Action* (1973 edn.), pp. 11, 19.

with *Anarchy*, it was not until after the success of *Tenants Take Over*, published by the Architectural Press in 1974, that Freedom Press suggested that he write a book for them. The result was *Housing: An Anarchist Approach*, which, to some extent, did recycle his *War Commentary* and *Freedom* pieces on postwar squatting.

Ward's difference of emphasis is, in part, to be explained that he was approaching anarchism from a background of architecture, town planning, the Garden City movement—"You could see the links between Ebenezer Howard and Kropotkin"—and regional planning. He was considerably influenced by Patrick Geddes (who is acknowledged in *Influences*), Lewis Mumford, and the regionalist approach. William Morris was also important but not for his political lectures, which were not to Ward's taste, but rather as mediated by the Arts and Crafts Movement (his early employer, Sidney Caulfield, had actually known Morris) and, in particular, by Lethaby. It is Alexander Herzen, though not an anarchist, whom he regards as his principal political influence—

> A goal which is infinitely remote is not a goal at all, it is a deception. A goal must be closer—at the very least the labourer's wage or pleasure in the work performed. Each epoch, each generation, each life has had, or has, its own experience, and the end of each generation must be itself.[20]

—and by extension Herzen's outstanding expositor in English, Isaiah Berlin, whose major liberal statements, *Historical Inevitability* and *Two Concepts of Liberty*, he also prizes. George Orwell and his "pretty anarchical"

---

20   Quoted in *Anarchy in Action* (1973 edn.), p. 136.

version of socialism also need to be mentioned; indeed a series of five articles by Ward on "Orwell and Anarchism," first published in 1955 in *Freedom*, were reprinted in *George Orwell at Home (and among the Anarchists)* (1998).

From across the Atlantic two periodicals, available from Freedom Bookshop, were important: *Politics* (1944–49), edited by Dwight Macdonald in the course of his transition from Marxism to a pacifist anarchism, Ward considered "my ideal of a political journal," admiring its "breadth, sophistication, dryness" (although Macdonald worked in London in the 1950s and 1960s Ward was only to meet him two or three times); and *Why?* (1942–47), later *Resistance* (1947–52), edited by a group which included David Wieck and Paul Goodman. Goodman, who also contributed to *Politics*, was another principal influence, firstly and always, for *Communitas* (1947), the planning classic he wrote with his brother Percival, but also for the very similar anarchism to Ward's he began to expound from "The May Pamphlet," included in *Art and Social Nature* (1946), onwards. Goodman became a frequent contributor to *Anarchy* and *Anarchy in Action* is dedicated to his memory; yet Ward was only to meet him once—when he was in London in 1967 for the Dialectics of Liberation conference. In *Anarchy 33* Ward had drawn attention to the similarities between Goodman and Alex Comfort, and the Comfort of *Authority and Delinquency in the Modern State* (1950) and *Delinquency* (1951), in which he calls for anarchism to become a libertarian action sociology, is the final significant influence on Ward's anarchism.

Ward was, with good reason, scornful of most other anarchists' obsession with the history, whether glorious or infamous, of their tradition: "I think the besetting sin of anarchism has been its preoccupation with its own past . . ."[21] Still, despite his own emphasis on the here-and-now and the future, he wrote four historical books: (with Dennis Hardy) *Arcadia for All: The Legacy of a Makeshift Landscape* (1984); (also with Dennis Hardy) *Goodnight Campers! The History of the British Holiday Camp* (1986); (with David Crouch) *The Allotment: Its Landscape and Culture* (1988); and *Cotters and Squatters: Housing's Hidden History* (2002). The masterly *Arcadia for All*, a history of the "plotlands" of South-East England, is simply a natural extension back into the recent past of his major interest in self-build and squatting in the present; and *The Allotment* touches upon similar issues. In *Goodnight Campers!* the entrepreneurial holiday camps are traced to their origins in the early 20th century and the "pioneer camps," in which a key role was played by the major organisations of working-class self-help and mutual aid, the co-operative movement and trade unions. The historic importance of such institutions in the provision of welfare and the maintenance of social solidarity was to become after *Goodnight Campers!* a theme of increasing significance in Ward's work. He stated his case in "The Path Not Taken," a striking short article of 1987; but his analysis over the next ten years has fleshed out and developed a longstanding preoccupation. Since the late 19th century "the tradition of fraternal and autonomous associations springing up from below" has been successively displaced by one of "authoritarian institutions directed from above."[22] He sees a "sinister alliance of Fabians and Marxists, both of whom believed implicitly in the state, and assumed that they

---

21    "Colin Ward Interview," *Freedom*, June 1984.
22    Colin Ward, "The Path Not Taken," *The Raven*, no. 3 (November 1987), p. 195—where he says these phrases, which also appear in *Anarchy in Action* (1973 edn.), p. 123, were first published in 1956 in *Freedom* (but the original printing is actually located in a long letter of 30 June 1960 to the *Listener*).

would be the particular elite in control of it effectively combining with "the equally sinister alliance of bureaucrats and professionals: the British civil service and the British professional classes, with their undisguised contempt for the way ordinary people organised anything." The result was that: "The great tradition of working-class self-help and mutual aid was written off not just as irrelevant, but as an actual impediment, by the political and professional architects of the welfare state . . . The contribution that the recipients had to make . . . was ignored as a mere embarrassment . . ."[23] Drawing upon several recent historical works, he was able to show that the 19th-century dame schools, set up by working-class parents for working-class children and under working-class control, were swept away by the board schools of the 1870s; and similarly the self-organization of patients in the working-class medical societies was to be lost in the creation of the National Health Service. Ward commented from his own specialism on the initially working-class self-help building societies stripping themselves of the final vestiges of mutuality; and this degeneration has existed alongside a tradition of municipal housing that was adamantly opposed to the principle of dweller control. Here we are presented with a rich, never more relevant, analysis of the disaster of modern British social policy with pointers to the way ahead if we are to stand any chance of reinstituting the self-organization and mutual aid that have been lost. He restated his argument in *Social Policy: An Anarchist Response*, his 1996 lectures at the London School of Economics which summarise several of his most important themes.

Down to his death in February 2010, Colin Ward saw anarchism's best prospects in the immediate future

---

23  Ward, "The Path Not Taken," p. 196.

as lying within the environmental and ecological movement. One of his greatest regrets remained that so few
anarchists follow his example and apply their principles
to what they themselves know best. In his case that was
the terrain of housing, architecture, and planning; but
where, he wanted to know, are the anarchist experts on,
and applicators to, for example, medicine, the health service, agriculture, and economics?

*David Goodway*

# TALKING ANARCHY

*First, and most obviously, tell me how you became an anarchist*

I came from a Labour Party family in one of the eastern suburbs of London and I knew about the existence of anarchism because of the Spanish war. My father was the youngest of a family of ten children from the East India Dock Road, where his father was described as a "general dealer." In his early teens he became a "pupil teacher" at the school he attended and subsequently won a place at a teacher-training college. After the First World War, while teaching in the London docklands, he earned a degree in geography at the London School of Economics, one of the few institutions catering for that kind of part-time study. My mother was the daughter of a carpenter from the same area of London.

I passed what was known as the scholarship examination to the local high school, but left at the end of the fourth year at fifteen in 1939. I must have been a disappointment to my parents, and I am sure that my father felt that, if I was not capable of the sustained effort that he had imposed on himself, there was no point in pushing me to succeed. One of my big interests as a boy was in printing (of the now obsolete kind, with moveable metal type). I bought an old treadle-operated press, and a friend of my brother who worked for a newspaper used to bring home parcels of old type for me. Later, when I wanted to show him the results of his kindness, I learned that he had been killed in an air raid.

I failed to find a job in the printing trade, but my third job, in 1941, was working on the drawing board for an elderly architect whose own history went back to William Morris and the Arts and Crafts Movement of the 1890s. His own work had dwindled to temporary repairs to factories in the East End of London, very familiar to me, which had been destroyed in the blitz of September 1940.

But, like any young worker, in the centre of London for the first time, I spent a lot of time exploring the city itself, and remember discovering the Socialist Book Centre in Essex Street, off the Strand, run by Orwell's friend Jon Kimche. It was there that I discovered Orwell's writings, hard to find elsewhere, and journals like *Tribune* and the *New Leader*.

Like any other eighteen-year-old (for I knew no war-resisters), I was conscripted into the army in 1942 and, because of my occupation, was automatically sent to join the Royal Engineers. I was taught how to build bridges and how to make explosions, but there must have been a sudden shortage of draughtsmen because, in the extraordinary way that military strategy works, I was sent to the Army School of Hygiene, to make large-scale drawings of latrines and of deadly insects, as a guide to camp builders and sanitary engineers.

Then, in the autumn of 1943, the same vagaries of military strategy sent me to Glasgow in Scotland, to work in a requisitioned mansion in Park Terrace with a wonderful panorama of the smoky city below us, where heavy industry was booming for the first time since the First World War. My Sundays were free, and I would spend them exploring the city, and its wonderful, free, and open-on-Sundays Mitchell Library, until it was time to hear the open-air political orators. Glasgow had a long tradition of political oratory, and at this time anarchism was represented by two remarkably witty and sardonic speakers, Eddie Shaw and Jimmie Dick. They handed out leaflets directing us to the anarchist bookshop in George Street and the nearby meeting room above the Hangman's Rest pub in Wilson Street.

*They were working men, weren't they, and, ideologically, managed to combine individualism and syndicalism?*

Yes, you are right. Both the propagandists I mentioned linked the most apparently incompatible versions of anarchism. But for me, the most impressive of the Glasgow anarchists was Frank Leech. He was an Irishman, not from Ireland, but from Lancashire in England, a Navy boxing champion in the First World War. He had a general shop in one of the housing estates on the fringe of the city. There he had housed refugees from Germany and from Spain, and operated a printing press. When I told him about the material from official American publications that I had read in the Mitchell Library describing plans for postwar Europe, he urged me to put it together in articles for the London publication *War Commentary—for Anarchism*, and to post them to Mrs. M.L. Richards. This I did, and the material appeared in, I think, December 1943.

By that time Frank Leech was in trouble with the law and was anxious to make propaganda out of staging a hunger strike in Barlinnie Prison. He was a much-loved character, and his friends, worried about his health, urged me to attempt to visit him at the prison to persuade him to abandon his hunger strike. They thought that a soldier in uniform, with a London rather than a Glasgow accent, would be more likely to be admitted by the prison governor. My visit to the prison was evidently noted, because immediately afterwards I was posted by the army to a maintenance unit in the Orkney and Shetland Islands at the extreme North-East of Scotland.

There is an irony here. My suspected unreliability kept me in safety for the rest of the war, while many other conscripts of my generation died in forgotten and meaningless battles in South-East Asia.

But I had been won for anarchism by the busy self-educated Glasgow propagandists, who had put me in touch with their bookshop, selling the range of available anarchist literature and, by post, with the Freedom Press Bookshop in London.

*Why did anarchism so appeal, at a time when enthusiasm for Soviet Communism was at its zenith?*

I am not quite sure how I managed not to be swept up into the Stalin-worship that infected the British Left. But the literature on sale at the anarchist bookshop in Glasgow included the writings of Emma Goldman and Alexander Berkman. Frank Leech himself printed and published Emma Goldman's pamphlet *Trotsky Protests Too Much*. I was influenced very early by the writings of Arthur Koestler and George Orwell. Lilian Wolfe, a veteran from earlier years of Freedom Press, put me on her mailing list for copies of several dissident journals, like for example, Dwight Macdonald's *Politics* from 1944, whose common factor was hostility to the blanket Stalinism of the regular left-wing press. Also in 1944, Freedom Press first published Marie Louise Berneri's book *Workers in Stalin's Russia*, reprinting several times in the postwar years. It argued that the fundamental test of any political regime was "How do the workers fare under it?" and that, by this test, the Soviet regime was a disaster, with the same extremes of wealth and poverty as the capitalist world. It appeared at a time when there was a tacit agreement in the British press not to criticise the Soviet Union. I am certain that later generations will never be able to comprehend how deeply Marxist and Stalinist ideas had circumscribed the assumptions of the British and Western European intelligentsia.

*How would you account for this quasi-religious infatuation?*

It really was like a religious conversion for many people: the search for ultimate certainties. Probably it was Orwell who described it as "transferred patriotism," meaning that people who had rejected unconditional loyalty to the country of their birth, applied it, like an adhesive plaster, to a different country. You could see this in the post-war decades, where British Marxists, prised away from Stalin-worship, applied their loyalty to Tito's Yugoslavia, and when disillusioned there, immediately shifted it to Castro's Cuba. I know of no weapon against this, except ridicule.

*How do you define anarchism? Are you a socialist? Does your anarchism include that of the syndicalists, individualists, pacifists, and so on?*

To define anarchism I always adopt the opening words of the article on anarchism that Kropotkin wrote for the eleventh edition of the *Encyclopaedia Britannica* in 1905, where he explains that it is "the name given to a principle or theory of life and conduct under which society is conceived without government—harmony in such a society being obtained, not by submission to law, or by obedience to any authority, but by free agreements concluded between the various groups, territorial and professional, freely constituted for the sake of production and consumption, as also for the satisfaction of the infinite variety of needs and aspirations of a civilised being."

I am in complete agreement with the definition that Kropotkin expands from this preliminary statement. This means that I am, by definition, a socialist or what Kropotkin would have called an anarchist communist. But equally, I would always stress the common ground between people who have arrived at anarchist attitudes from different starting points. I think that the Freedom Press Group of the wartime years brought together people from all the tendencies you mention, and I think that this was characteristic of the people connected with *Freedom* all though its history.

I actually mistrust those anarchists who spend their time demolishing the contentions of another anarchist faction.

*I certainly take your point, yet I must press you on this issue. I don't see any reference to socialism—the common ownership of the means of production, distribution, and exchange—in the definition you have adopted from Kropotkin.*

That is because most of the varieties of socialism that we know about involve the activities of central or local government. But the co-operative movement around the world illustrates a variety of forms of common ownership of the means of production, distribution, and exchange, without dependence on the state.

*Of course, yet I consider Kropotkin's definition to be of anarchism only, and not of socialism—even if it may have socialist implications. How do you, personally, relate to syndicalism?*

Workers' control of industrial production seems to me to be the only approach compatible with anarchism, so I am automatically a supporter of syndicalist aims. But on the other hand, I have frequently seen the attempts by a militant minority to push minor disputes into an ultimate struggle, inevitably losing majority support and causing ordinary workers to *fear* militancy. Syndicalists, just like novelists and social critics, tended to exaggerate the extent to which manufacturing industry was dominated by vast Ford-type factories, organized with military precision, when, as Kropotkin stressed a hundred years ago, the typical workplace is a small workshop. Probably, when syndicalists succeed in abandoning historical romanticism, they will be exploiting the new communications technology to fight international capitalism on an international scale.

*And individualism?*

I scarcely need to tell you that the most individualistic people I have known have been people who rejected ideologies of individualism, and firmly believed in communist anarchism. I don't say this as a joke but as an everyday observation.

*And pacifism?*

Once again, I have watched different generations of anarchists adopting attitudes on violence and non-violence.

I remember a delightful old Irish anarchist from many years ago, Matt Kavanagh, who used to say (with reference to people known to you and me) "The trouble with pacifists is that they'll punch you on the nose, without a second thought!" But for people who see modern pacifism as a naïve or simplistic approach, I would recommend the book by my friend Michael Randle, on *Civil Resistance* (London: Fontana, 1994), discussing the potentialities and the limitations of pacifist action.

I am sure that George Orwell, who devoted plenty of time in the Second World War to attacking the pacifist standpoint of his friends like Alex Comfort and George Woodcock, observed, in spite of this, that the people who most readily attack the ideology of non-violence are those with little experience of the ugliness, squalidness, and arbitrary nature of violence.

*For all your adult life you have been associated with the Freedom Press in London. Would you tell me something of its history?*

The first issue of *Freedom* was produced in October 1886 by a remarkable woman, Charlotte Wilson, who had corresponded with Kropotkin and his wife, Sophie, urging them to come to England after his release from prison in France in January 1886. His fame and her organizational ability resulted in a journal based on the model of Kropotkin's experience with *Le Révolté* from Geneva in 1878 and *La Révolte* in Paris in 1885.

The paper they started survived despite police raids and imprisonments in the First World War until, in 1928, Tom Keell, who had been the self-effacing editor since 1907, retired from London with his companion Lilian Wolfe to Whiteway Colony, a Tolstoyan commune in the

West of England, that had been a refuge for anarchists since it was founded in 1898.

While issuing a *Freedom Bulletin* for the surviving subscribers, Keell was watching for signs of a renewal of anarchist propaganda. This came in 1936 when he was approached by Vernon Richards, the son of a veteran London Italian anarchist, Emidio Recchioni (1864–1934), who had a famous grocery shop, "King Bomba," at 37 Old Compton Street in Soho. Vero, his original name which all his friends used, started a journal, *Free Italy*, superseded after the events of July 1936 by *Spain and the World*, and Tom Keell rejoiced that there was a new home for the ideas and the old pamphlets he was storing. As the struggle in Spain dwindled to its end in 1939, the journal's name was changed, first to *Revolt!* and then to *War Commentary: for Anarchism,* its title reverting to *Freedom* in 1945. In 1943, Lilian Wolfe, who had been running a food shop in Stroud, Gloucestershire, abandoned it at the age of sixty-seven, in order to manage the office of Freedom Press in London. She died at ninety-eight in 1974, and Nicolas Walter explained how "For more than twenty-five years Lilian Wolfe was the centre of the administration of Freedom Press at its various premises in London. She was the person on whom every organization depends—the completely reliable worker who runs the office, opening and closing the shop, answering the telephone and the post, doing accounts and keeping people in touch. She maintained personal contact with the thousands of people who read the paper . . ." This was certainly true in my case. When I wrote, obscurely, from a military address, she would reply and would send me copies of journals from overseas, like *La Protesta* from Buenos Aires and *L'Adunata* from New York.

*Am I right in thinking, however, that you first actually met the Freedom Press Group when they were in the dock at the Central Criminal Court in London, and you were in the witness box as a witness for the prosecution?*

Yes, this is true. Of all the European countries involved in the Second World War, Britain was the one in which it was easiest for opponents of the war to survive. When, after the war I met anarchists from France, the Netherlands, and Italy, they expressed amazement at the tolerance, in Britain, of dissent. As someone who had submitted to conscription into the army, I had no experience of this, although I later met people whose evasion of military service resulted in continual persecution and imprisonment. There were few journals who were totally opposed to the war aims of all the combatant nations, so *War Commentary* was an obvious candidate for the attention of the Special Branch (the name then given to the British Government's secret police), but it was not until the last year of the war that serious persecution began.

In November 1944, John Olday, the paper's cartoonist, was arrested and, after a protracted trial, was sent to prison for twelve months for "stealing by finding an identity card." He declined to give evidence and consequently had to be imprisoned on a technicality. A reader called T.W. Brown had been jailed earlier for distributing "seditious" leaflets. When he was sentenced at the Central Criminal Court, the government prosecutor had drawn attention to the fact that his penalty could have been fourteen years.

On 12 December 1944, officers of the Special Branch raided the Freedom Press office and the homes of editors and sympathisers. They were acting under Defence Regulation 38b, which declared that "no person should seduce members of the armed forces from their duty," and at the end of December, Special Branch officers, led by Inspector Whitehead, searched the belongings of soldiers in various parts of Britain. Purely by chance, I was in a Military Detention Camp at the time. This was for the crime of "refusing an order" but was really a matter of a "demarcation dispute" as trade-unionists would call it. I was required to do work appropriate to a qualified person, which I was not and consequently declined. Simply to embarrass my commanding officer, I pushed the issue as far as a court-martial!

I miscalculated and had to be escorted back from the prison camp on the island of South Ronaldsay to my own army unit at Stromness, Orkney, with two armed guards from the Military Police. It was like the adventures of the Good Soldier Schweik. In my presence the commanding officer searched my belongings and my mail, and retained various books and papers.

Soon afterwards, I was released from detention, and applied for the return of my property. My commanding officer said he had no authority to return it, and a few days later I was sent for to be interviewed by Inspector Whitehead. I wrote to Lilian Wolfe, telling her about these events, but mail from the Orkney Islands was censored and (as I learned later) the greater part of my letter was obliterated by the censor. I had written another letter and had persuaded a civilian to post it on the mainland of Scotland. This was later passed back to me for identification when I was a witness at the Freedom Press trial. Years later, this letter and other items taken from me, including the offending issues of the newspapers, were returned to me, and I noted that what I had written to Lilian was:

> Whitehead drew my attention to the article "All Power to the Soviets" in the November *War*

*Commentary*, and to the duplicated *Freedom Press Forces Letter* of about the same date, and asked if I had read them. I said "Yes." He pointed to one paragraph in the article, referring to the revolutionary effect of Soldiers' Councils in Russia in 1917, and to a paragraph in the letter, which asked its readers in general terms about the existence and use of Soldiers' Councils. He asked what conclusion I drew from these two articles in conjunction, and whether I considered them an incitement to mutiny. I gave a non-committal reply . . .

Meanwhile, in January 1945, Philip Sansom, one of the *Freedom* editors, was sent to prison for two months "for being in possession of an army waterproof coat and for failing to notify a change of address." There was an evident determination to put the editors of *War Commentary* out of circulation. On 22 February 1945, Marie Louise Berneri, Vernon Richards, and John Hewetson were arrested at 7:30 in the morning and were charged with offences under the Defence Regulations. In court, they were joined by Philip Sansom who had been brought from Brixton Prison. They appeared four times at the Magistrate's Court before their trial occupied four days at the Central Criminal Court. It was held before a celebrated judge, Sir Norman Birkett, and the prosecution was conducted by the Attorney General. In the last days of the Second World War, on 26 April 1945, Richards, Hewetson, and Sansom were found guilty and each of them was sentenced to nine months' imprisonment. Marie Louise Berneri was found not guilty and was discharged on a technicality, which infuriated her. She had married Vernon Richards (in order to acquire the right to live in Britain), and her defence counsel had simply to indicate that, in English law, since husband and wife are legally one person, a wife cannot be accused of conspiracy with her husband!

*Were they guilty of anything?*

The whole prosecution case was simply the approach laid down by Inspector Whitehead: to connect the circular letter sent to the hundred or so members of the armed forces who were subscribers to *War Commentary* with various articles on the history of soldiers' councils in Russia and Germany in 1917 and 1918, and on the situation in European resistance movements which, as the Allied armies advanced in 1944, were being told to hand over their weapons to the governments then being imposed under military auspices. One of the headlines in *War Commentary*, for example, demanded "Hold on to your Arms!." This was used by the prosecution to show that the paper was urging British soldiers to keep their rifles for possible revolutionary action. The article was, in fact—and the context made this clear—addressed to the Belgian underground, after the German army had withdrawn, but before a new regime had been imposed upon them. The whole of the prosecution's "evidence" was as flimsy as this. The four soldiers called by the prosecution (including me) to establish that the offending material had been received by them, testified for the defence that they had not been disaffected.

The accused editors (who incidentally could be shown on stylistic grounds not to be the authors of the circular letters sent to soldiers) disliked the way in which their case was presented. But if the object of the whole procedure was to silence the Freedom Press, it would have been foolish to strike intransigent attitudes and get, in consequence, far longer sentences. The crime of disaffecting members of the armed forces from their duty carried a fourteen-year penalty. As it was, they were given shorter sentences than T.W. Brown or John Olday, whose "crimes" were much more trivial. In fact, Marie Louise and George Woodcock were able to keep the paper running while their comrades were in jail.

The National Council for Civil Liberties (now called Liberty) served as a pressure group in cases like the Freedom Press trial, but at this particular period in its history it had fallen under Communist control and spent its time demanding that the British Fascist, Sir Oswald Mosley, who had spent most of the war in prison, should be re-arrested. So a Freedom Press Defence Committee was organised by the surrealist Simon Watson Taylor, and it won the support of public figures from Bertrand Russell to George Orwell and Benjamin Britten. Subsequently, it became the Freedom Defence Committee raising issues like the treatment of deserters or the internment of Spanish refugees as prisoners of war. It achieved their release.

*You were belatedly released from the army in 1947 and you were immediately asked to join the Freedom Press Group, weren't you? Who were the most important figures of this extremely talented group and how did they influence you?*

They certainly were an extremely talented group, and they made a deep impression on me, becoming lifelong friends. I had the opportunity to meet them all at parties held to welcome the imprisoned editors on their release. Early in 1946, I was moved from Orkney (no longer a threat to national security) to another unit of the Royal Engineers, camped on a polo ground in South-West London, where our task was to dig latrines for the soldiers, sailors, and airmen taking part in a Victory Parade in Hyde Park (which had been populated by sheep all through the war.) This enabled me to write a series of reports on the squatters' movement that emerged, with the seizure by homeless families of empty military camps, but also to attend the meetings organised by the London Anarchist Group and by the Freedom Defence Committee, which was organizing meetings to focus attention on the plight of at least a hundred refugees from the Spanish war, who had been used as forced labour during the German occupation of France, and were treated by the British as prisoners of war and imprisoned in Lancashire.

The key figures were undoubtedly Vero and Marie Louise, simply because they had been involved with the task of producing an anarchist journal since 1936, when he was aged twenty-one, and she since she came to live in England in 1937 at the age of eighteen, after her father was murdered in Barcelona. Their knowledge of international anarchism, its trends and personalities, as well, of course, as their easy use of four languages, added weight to their opinions.

Vero had great charm and relished the art of cooking delicious meals with simple ingredients. He had trained as a civil engineer and until his arrest had been working on railway building. His conversation on railway design was fascinating, although he never wrote on the subject. Sadly, he has died, at the age of eighty-six, during the course of our conversations. I have always regretted that I was never able to persuade him to write about the aspects of life, whether as a city child, or about railways or horticulture, where he had direct personal experience to share.

And of course *everyone* fell in love with Marie Louise. There is a famous English diarist, Frances Partridge, who on 22 January 1941 described a visit to the writer Gerald

Brenan and his wife: "They had staying with them their Italian anarchist friend, Maria Luisa, wife of the son of King Bomba, the Soho grocer. She is, I think, the most beautiful girl I ever saw, and with this goes great sweetness, a low husky voice and apparent intelligence." And when Lewis Mumford, himself the author of a survey of utopias, reviewed Marie Louise's *Journey Through Utopia*, he found it to be "such a book as only a brave intelligence and an ardent spirit can produce."

I have very few personal memories of Marie Louise. One is of an occasion when we met for lunch in a very ordinary Greek restaurant, to eat a dish of *moussaka* and discuss the importance of William Morris. She behaved as though this prosaic meal was a special occasion, which of course it was for me. I knew her for only two years, and I have often wondered about the books she might have written but for the tragedy of her death at the age of thrity-one in 1949.

Another immensely useful member of the Freedom Press Group in those days was George Woodcock. He was born in Canada in 1912 and had been brought to England as a child. In 1949 he returned to Canada, where he became one of that country's best-known writers. He had begun the Second World War as a pacifist and had started a literary magazine *NOW* in 1940, and in 1942 had become one of the busy writers and editors of *War Commentary*.

He was by far the most prolific of the new pamphleteers, writing a series of pamphlets in that area where anarchist propaganda in English, and probably in other languages, has been weakest: the application of anarchist ideas to specific social issues. I was drawn to his writing because among these was his study of *Railways and Society* and his pamphlet on housing *Homes or Hovels*? But especially important for me was his study of regionalism in a series of articles in *Freedom* (later subsumed, I suppose, in his biography of Kropotkin) where he made the connections between the French regional geographers like Reclus, by way of Kropotkin and Patrick Geddes, with Ebenezer Howard's decentralist ideology and the Regional Planning Association of America and the work of Lewis Mumford. George died in 1995 in Vancouver.

John Hewetson (1913–1990) came to anarchism from the Forward Movement, a radical break-away from the pacifist Peace Pledge Union, and began writing for *War Commentary* in 1942. He was a physician who at the time of his arrest was Casualty Officer at Paddington Hospital. After his release from prison, he spent his entire working life as a general practitioner in poor districts of London. He was a pioneer of advocacy of freely available contraception and abortion and of enlightened attitudes to drug users.

Philip Sansom (1916–1999) came from the same part of London as I did, and trained as a commercial artist at West Ham Technical College. He was working on the land as a conscientious objector to military service, when in 1943 he discovered the London anarchists, as well as the surrealists. In *War Commentary* and then in *Freedom*, he was both industrial editor and a sharply witty cartoonist.

He designed the jackets of many Freedom Press publications, from John Hewetson's *Ill-Health, Poverty and the State* onward, and was responsible for some masterly typographical covers for Freedom pamphlets. In the post-war years he was working at the print-shop where the paper was produced, and I vividly remember two occasions when he telephoned me at work to ask if he could print extra copies of articles of mine to distribute as leaflets from his speaker's platform at Hyde Park. I, of course, felt enormously flattered by his request, and was even more gratified when he asked me to write the "Publisher's Foreword" to his pamphlet on *Syndicalism: The Workers' Next Step*. Open-hearted generosity was a characteristic of Philip, and I always associate him with laughter and impromptu songs.

Another member of the Freedom Press Group when I joined it was John Olday (1904–1977) whose cartoons for the journal were collected in the book *The March to Death*, where they were accompanied by news items from the wartime press selected by Marie Louise. This was originally published in 1943 and was recently reprinted. He grew up in Hamburg, the son of an English father and a German mother (his original name was Arthur William Oldag), and was a member of *Wandervogel*-type movements among the young in pre-Nazi Germany and of subsequent anti-Nazi struggles. His activities were known to the authorities in Germany and he used his dual nationality to get to England in 1938, where he published an autobiography, *Kingdom of Rags* (London: Jarrold, 1938), and in 1939 volunteered for the British army. He deserted from the army, with the result that other members of the Freedom Group had the embarrassing task of dumping his rifle, a long-barrelled Lee-Enfield, in the nearest canal without being observed. (These were the people imprisoned by the government for urging soldiers to hold on to their arms!) Olday was a charming man who told me about the folklore of German revolutionaries like Max Hölz, and taught me a few chords on the guitar. He had a marvellous repertoire of folksongs from North Germany which I was not to hear again for forty years, when they were sung to us by Ruth, the German partner of our son Tom. In the early 1950s, John Olday emigrated to Australia, but returned in the 1970s to perform in the gay cabaret scene in Germany and Britain.

Yet another member was Gerald Vaughan, who must have been working on the land, as he wrote the "Land Notes" column very well in *Freedom*. He seemed to have stopped doing so at the end of the 1940s, since I have a few cuttings of items by me (as the universal emergency journalist) under this heading. I associate him with the painter Pip Walker, who I remember with her troop of delightful children in an idyllic part of London, the Vale of Health, in Hampstead. Later she was the partner of the poet, printer, and publisher Asa Benveniste, whose grave, with its touching inscription, "He had the misfortune to be a poet," you showed to us at Heptonstall in Yorkshire.

The next person to be asked to join the group, after me, was Rita Milton. She and I are the same age and we are, sad to say, the last survivors of the Freedom Group from those days. She is the daughter of a well-known left-wing Scottish nationalist, Alexander Inglis Milton, and, like me, was attracted toward anarchism by the Glasgow open-air orators, Eddie Shaw and Jimmy Dick. She says that she came down from there to London for an Anarchist Summer School, met Philip Sansom, and decided to stay in the South. Like him, she was a brilliant outdoor orator, at Hyde Park and at Tower Hill in London. At the second of these open-air pulpits, the famous Christian socialist propagandist, Dr. Donald Soper, always described her as his favorite anarchist. Rita and I rotated for years in the first fortnightly, and then weekly, task of processing the *Freedom* wrappers through the addressing machine, one of the many routine tasks eliminated by new technologies.

My colleagues in the Freedom Group influenced me greatly, not only about the interpretation of anarchism, but also about most other things. You must remember that I had been in the army from the age of eighteen to that of twenty-three, much of that time spent in a remote part of Britain, and was suddenly part of, by my standards, a sophisticated and cosmopolitan milieu. One of these new joys was food, and especially the French and Italian cuisine. Naturally, when working in central London, I introduced my architectural colleagues to the King Bomba shop, where the always smiling Eugenio Celoria would give them cooking suggestions as he wrapped their purchases.

Another was music. Like most English children of my generation, I had been educated in music by the BBC, and it was a joy to have friends like Vero and John Hewetson who would discuss the chamber music of Beethoven, Haydn, and Mozart, and the operas of Verdi with immense enthusiasm, rushing to the gramophone to illustrate the arguments from their big collections of 78 rpm discs. Unlike them, I was also, like Philip, a devotee of New Orleans jazz. In the late 1940s, Philip was working part-time, together with the jazz and blues singer George Melly, for the surrealist dealer E.L.T. Mesens at the London Gallery in Brook Street. George Melly, who is the same age as me, is still giving pleasure to jazz audiences and never fails to declare his allegiance to anarchism. He was brought to anarchist ideas by the penny pamphlet by George Woodcock, *What is Anarchism?,* when he was in the Navy.

But perhaps the most important influence on me from the Freedom Press Group was in its attitudes to sexual freedom and enlightenment. This was most certainly not on the agenda of any other political group, least of all the Marxists. Marie Louise's article "Sexuality and Freedom" in George Woodcock's magazine *NOW* (No. 5, in 1945) was one of the earliest discussions anywhere in the British press of the theories of Wilhelm Reich. And John Hewetson was a well-known pioneer among male doctors, both for freely available contraception and for abortion on demand. He, like Marie Louise, was also interested in the social importance of Wilhelm Reich's ideas. One of his partners in his National Health Service practice in London was Dr. Robert Ollendorf, the brother-in-law of Reich.

At an editorial meeting early in 1951, the question arose of how an anarchist paper should treat a topic that was dominating the headlines of the popular press: a wave of child murders with sexual overtones. John undertook the task of writing a series of articles on *Sexual Freedom for the Young*, which Freedom Press reprinted as a pamphlet.

John was arguing a case, familiar to most of us, that behind the adult offender, convicted of terrible crimes, there is a lonely, unloved, and sexually repressed child. The most remarkable thing about his pamphlet was its date. It is hard to convey to readers in the 21st century that, in the 1950s in Britain, sex was a generally taboo subject still, and that to discuss the sexuality of children was to risk prosecution for obscenity. It is one measure of the distance we have travelled since then that it now seems absurd that this, or indeed Alex Comfort's Freedom Press book of 1948, *Barbarism and Sexual Freedom*, should have been seen as "risky" publications. It was John who evoked something of the spirit of the Freedom Press Group of those days, many years later. Early in 1990, the year of his death, he wrote to Philip Sansom:

> I must write you a line after the fall of Ceaucescu. The events of the last six months in Europe seem incredible—we have been drinking to the damnation and destruction of these Marxist-Leninist regimes all our lives—back to Marie Louise's times. Orwell thought they were so ruthlessly defended

that they couldn't be brought down and now suddenly they have collapsed like the walls of Jericho!

How we would have celebrated if we had all been together as we were in the '40s. And how I would have loved to be laughing excitedly with Marie Louise . . .

Drink a glass with me and George not only to the damnation of the Stalinist shits, but to the old times that were so good!

*Would you give me some idea of the Group's way of life? I'm thinking of producing* Freedom*; selling* Freedom*; public meetings and oratory; friendships and relationships; summer schools and camps and holidays; children; families; and education; and the relation between the central core and a wider group of supporters and sympathisers.*

When I was invited to join the Freedom Press Group in 1947, it had leased the Freedom Bookshop in central London and had bought the Express Printers in an alley off Whitechapel High Street in the East End. Editorial meetings, every two weeks, were held either in the room behind the bookshop or at the home of Vero and Marie Louise at Chalk Farm, or of John Hewetson and Peta Edsall, first in Hampstead, and after 1948 in Vauxhall Bridge Road and then Southwark Bridge Road, above John's consulting room. Meetings were merry, social occasions, where Lilian Wolfe who ran the bookshop and coped with the mail, would persuade group members to deal with correspondence that needed more than an answer from her, and to accept or reject incoming articles and letters intended for publication. Current events were discussed and responsibility to write about them was distributed around the group.

Most of us knew, or learned, how to mark up material for the typesetter, how to correct proofs, and how to paste-up the "dummy" of the paper ready for Mr. Anderson, the elderly compositor, to insert the headlines, and Ben Chandler, the machinist, to print the paper on the very old printing press that Freedom Press had acquired in 1942 when it became hard to find a printer ready to undertake its work. Within the group there was absolute trust. We did not read each other's contributions to check on their ideological acceptability.

Most of us developed some experience of indoor and outdoor speaking, but the two outstanding speakers with the group were Philip and Rita, and at Hyde Park Lilian and other friends would sell the paper in the street. There were weekly indoor meetings organised by the London Anarchist Group, because, as you suggest, the existence of a bookshop with a stock of anarchist "classics," and a fortnightly paper (weekly after 1951) and open-air speakers, meant that there were networks of anarchists in a city the size of London who could engage in, or stay aloof from, the activities of Freedom Press . . .

*That's an interesting remark! Who stayed aloof?*

I think it is inevitable, rather than interesting. To the outside world, anarchism, like Trotskyism, makes itself ridiculous because of its ideological subdivisions. I remember Dwight Macdonald describing the New York dissident Marxists who were divided into a brigade of small sects, one of which was the Weisbordites which lost supporters, one by one, "until the Revolutionary League of America—the title made up in scope for any restriction of numbers—consisted of the leader and his wife. Then there was a divorce, and the advance-guard of the revolution was concentrated, like a *bouillon* cube, in the small person of Albert Weisbord . . ." Various old individualists stayed away, because the reporting of both demonstrations and industrial disputes, by Philip and by several "genuine" workers, offended their individualism, and various syndicalists ignored *Freedom* for the same reason, even though Philip Sansom produced, paid for, and edited a supplement to the paper called *The Syndicalist*.

Vernon Richards had ignored the elderly Jewish anarchists of the Workers' Friend group in East London, because they had followed Rudolf Rocker's support of the Anglo-American cause in the Second World War. On the other hand, Philip and Rita and I always accepted their invitations. I remember speaking at their celebrations of both the 75th birthday and the centenary of Rocker. The Express Printers was one of the few places which retained printing type in the Yiddish language, and we formed warm friendships with, for example, the poet Avrom Stencl.[1] They no longer published their journal The Workers' Friend, but, like Freedom Press, distributed the New York *Fraye Arbeter Shtime* (Free Voice of Labour), which frequently translated my *Freedom* articles.

A later dissident from *Freedom* was Albert Meltzer, who when I knew him was a marvellously witty and well-informed conversationalist, who subsequently developed some kind of egomania, which our critics always tell us is the anarchist disease.

*But tell me more about the anarchist culture of the 1940s and 1950s.*

---

1    Editor of *Loshn un Lebn* magazine and author of *Fisherdorf* and other collections.

In the 1950s the idea of an anarchist club in central London was explored, and it started with a cellar in Holborn, not far from the Freedom Bookshop. By 1954 it had moved, as the Malatesta Club, to Percy Street, near Tottenham Court Road, an area where German, Russian, and Italian anarchists had settled almost a century earlier. Malatesta had lived there, working as an electrician. The club attracted traditional jazz and a long series of interesting speakers. My fondest recollections are of satirical songs devised and performed by Philip, accompanying himself by drumming on a cardboard box. The club died, after about four years, simply because of the escalation of rents in central London. We never had a tradition of the occupation of empty buildings to provide local social centres, except for "Tenants' Corner," a squatted building in South London which, for two decades, advised municipal tenants on the strategies for developing local co-operatives.

*And there were an anarchist school and anarchist Summer Schools . . .*

Yes, Burgess Hill School was a progressive school in North London, with several anarchists, Tony Weaver, Tony Gibson, and Marjorie Mitchell, on its teaching staff, and so far as I can remember, it was there that the first postwar Anarchist Summer School was held in 1947, followed by another at Liverpool in 1948, and again in 1949 in Glasgow and the Isle of Arran. Years later, one of the Glasgow anarchists of my generation, Robert Lynn, made a Summer School in that city into an annual event.

One of the organizers of that first Anarchist Summer School that I attended, was the psychologist Tony Gibson (1914–2001) who worked at Burgess Hill School, and went on to organise summer camps for both children and adults from 1946 to 1957. There was, in fact, more anarchist social life in London than the people whose Sundays were devoted to writing anarchist propaganda could possibly become engaged in.

For me, the most delightful survivor from the anarchist past was Matt Kavanagh who, like Lilian Wolfe, had been associated with *Freedom* since the years before the First World War, and who, of course, had spoken from the same platform as Malatesta, Kropotkin, Emma Goldman, and a host of legendary anarchist orators. At the beginning of the Second World War, Matt was living at Southend-on-Sea in Essex, where he was a regular and accomplished anarchist outdoor orator, and was continually threatened by the police under the Defence Regulations, which demanded the suppression of subversion.

Two Essex teenagers, Norman Potter and his brother, who adopted the name Louis Adeane, were attracted to anarchism by Matt. Louis became a poet and critic, writing for George Woodcock's magazine *NOW*. I used to meet him and his partner Pat Cooper in the early postwar years, but by 1951 they had moved to Cornwall in the South-West of England, and poor Louis died young in the 1970s. Norman Potter became a designer and maker of furniture and was the author of the book *What is a Designer?* which is seen as a key text. In the 1940s I would meet Norman and Caroline at the hospitable Hewetson household, but after that would see him only at about ten-yearly intervals when he would cajole me into addressing his students in London or Bristol or Plymouth. When he died, in 1995, his obituarists stressed how much he, just like me, owed to the Freedom Press Group. One of them, Robin Kinross, explained that, "It was within the British anarchist movement that he found a set of ideas and beliefs that would last his life. This was the cultured, internationalist anarchism of figures such as John Hewetson, Marie Louise Berneri, Vernon Richards and George Woodcock."

As an anarchist propagandist I have been interested for many years in the sociology of autonomous groups, and the Freedom Press Group as I first knew it seems to me to be an interesting example, having a secure internal network based on friendship and shared skills, and a series of external networks of contacts in a variety of fields. One of these, through John Hewetson, was with experiments in social medicine, like the Peckham Health Centre in South London; another was with experiments in education, like A.S. Neill's Summerhill School, where Marie Louise made a series of photographs, and with Burgess Hill School.

It was at Burgess Hill that I first met Herbert Read, who was one of that school's directors. His book *Poetry and Anarchism*, first published by Faber in 1938, and followed by his *The Philosophy of Anarchism*, from Freedom Press in 1940, were among the vital books whose influence led people of my generation, as well as those a little older, to describe themselves as anarchists. This is true of a great variety of readers including Murray Bookchin. When Philip Sansom was a student at West Ham in the 1930s, he and his fellow students were deeply influenced by Read's book *Art and Industry* which first appeared in 1934.

Shortly before Philip's death, I sent him your collection of essays on Read, *Herbert Read Reassessed* (Liverpool University Press, 1999), and he telephoned me to say, once again, that when he was drawn into the anarchist world in 1943 he was thrilled to find that his design guru was also an anarchist propagandist.

I first met Alex Comfort when I was still in the army, but was free to attend Sunday night meetings of the London Anarchist Group in 1946; and I met George

Orwell, drinking tea in an ante-room of the Holborn Hall in Grays Inn Road, when George Woodcock persuaded him to talk at a meeting to demand the release of those unfortunate Spaniards detained first by the Germans and then by the British in France, who were still interned in a prison camp in Lancashire.

*Read and Comfort were the best-known British anarchists of the time. How did you react to them as individuals? And what is your assessment of their work?*

Read was a quiet, gentle person and, if we ever met, I was hesitant to approach him because I knew he was continually harassed by unpublished poets or novelists who were soliciting his help in getting their great works published. My only concern was to ask his permission to reprint a broadcast of his in *Freedom* or *Anarchy*.

I valued Read because his anarchist propaganda reached a wider audience than most of us could expect. And his *Education Through Art*, together with his Freedom Press pamphlet on *The Education of Free Men*, were important, not for themselves, but for giving a climate of respectability to teachers I met, fighting on their own for the recognition of the role of the arts in education. In the late 1970s I was employed to propagate (among other things) the role of art in environmental education and I found Read's writings an important certificate of intellectual respectability.

You may smile, but this was very valuable to me at the time.

Relations with Alex Comfort were easier, because he had a jolly, joking nature. As you know, his first public advocacy of sexual freedom was in his Freedom Press book *Barbarism and Sexual Freedom*, in 1948, built around his lectures to the London Anarchist Group. No modern reader, half a century later, can appreciate the stifling sexual climate of ordinary life in those days, and can see how subtle a liberator Comfort was, in using ridicule to undermine authoritarian attitudes. What was important for me was his open approach to the lessons for all of us from the sociologists.

I have said nothing about either Read or Comfort as novelists or poets, because their importance for me is in their social ideas, not their "creative" writing.

But the fact that I belonged to the series of networks of contact and discussion which included them was one of the many ultimate results of the initiative at the end of 1936 of the twenty-one-year-old Vernon Richards in reviving anarchist publishing in London. As Philip Sansom explained it, in *Freedom*'s hundredth anniversary issue: "If Richards had not started *Spain and the World*, the whole history of modern British anarchism might have been not just different but non-existent, for that is where it stems from. And the British anarchist movement today, with all its various branches, has largely grown from the groups inspired by Freedom Press . . ."

*You once mentioned to me how small groups can have an influence entirely disproportionate to their actual numbers. You named, to my surprise, the French Impressionists as an example. Would you care to elaborate on this?*

Yes, I spoke of Alex Comfort's advice that we anarchists should learn from the sociologists. I took his advice more seriously than most of his admirers, and one of the documents I studied was the 1959 (final) issue of the American bulletin, *Autonomous Groups*, which contained an account of "The Batignolles Group—Creators of Impressionism" by Maria Rogers, and another of "The Old Gang, Nucleus of Fabianism" by Charles Kitzen.

The French Impressionists were a group of painters, mostly excluded by the Paris Salon, who included anarchists, for example Pissarro, and right-wingers, for example Degas. They formed an influential informal network built around the cafés where they met.

> In their meetings at the Café Guerbois, the painters expressed themselves freely, gained understanding of one another's aims, ideas, theories, and techniques, formulated criteria for judging their contemporaries, and jointly explored new influences . . .

The group, with its ever-widening circles of influence, disintegrated, but not before it had conquered the art market, and achieved recognition: the aim that brought them together in the first place.

In Britain, the nickname "the Old Gang" was given to a small group (George Bernard Shaw, Sidney and Beatrice Webb, Sydney Olivier, and Graham Wallas) who dominated the socialist organisation, the Fabian Society, from 1886 until 1911, and established the character of the Labour Party for most of the subsequent hundred years. Originally, the Society had held a wider view of socialism and had included the anarchist Charlotte Wilson, who in 1886 had, with Kropotkin, founded the journal *Freedom*. Obviously, as anarchists, we deplore the statist, bureaucratic version of socialism that the Fabian Old Gang bequeathed to Britain. They came together, initiated a program, and separated, not before achieving their original objective. Like the Impressionists, they exercised an influence far beyond their numbers. Both these groups, in totally different spheres of life were remarkably effective as autonomous groups.

*And their importance for anarchists?*

It is because, traditionally, anarchists have conceived of the whole of social organization as a series of interlocking networks of autonomous groups. So we should pay serious attention to studies of effective ones. In the journal *Anarchy* I twice drew attention to these particular studies. (In *Anarchy* no. 8, Oct 1961, pp. 230–231, and in *Anarchy*, no. 77, July 1967, pp. 206–208, where I condensed Dorothy Blitzen's conclusions from that bulletin *Autonomous Groups*.)

My personal experience of the dynamics of autonomous groups has been as a close observer of housing co-operatives in the 1970s, and as an active member of the Freedom Press Group from the late 1940s to the 1960s. Dr. Blitzen distinguished autonomous groups from other forms of organization associated with hierarchies of relationships, fixed divisions of labour, and explicit rules and practices.

In autonomous groups she noted "the degree of individual autonomy, the complete reliance on direct reciprocities for decisions for action affecting them all" which are not characteristic of larger organisations, and she observed "the flux of temporary leadership by one or another member." And she remarks that "it would be difficult to imagine a voluntary group made up of anything but peers. The range of inequality between members cannot be too great. Even in the instance of a voluntary association of a master and his students, the students manifest a fair repertoire of the master's skills, must approach or even equal his level of intelligence and, over time, narrow the gap between his abilities and theirs."

She also observed that in both the cases studied, the Impressionists and the Fabian "Old Gang," the groups began and ended with a series of friendships, while "similar interests, goals, skills, talents, or anything else, do not of themselves evoke associations. We often overlook the simple fact that people have to meet"; and she added that,

> It strikes me that autonomous groups do not so much promote friendship and sentiments that are friendly as organised them when circumstances bring them together, or particular goals required grouping for the achievement of particular ends. In the end, when the group no longer existed, the individuals and their friendships persisted.

One of the characteristics of those two disparate groups, the Impressionists and the Fabians, was that individual members provided links with a series of other specialist networks and interest groups. The Freedom Group in the days when I was asked to join it had links with the literary world through George Woodcock, with the world of the emergent Health Service and the field of contraception and sexual politics through John Hewetson, with the anarchist publishing groups in other languages through Marie Louise and Vero, with trade unionism and syndicalism through Philip, through several of us with the field of progressive education, and with me to those of architecture, housing, and planning.

These links were of lasting importance to me and they certainly affected the quality of *Freedom* and of Freedom Press publications.

*You developed a great empathy with all things Italian, didn't you? How did this originate?*

I explained to you how my connection with the Glasgow anarchists resulted in my being sent, from the end of 1943 until early 1946, to the Orkney and Shetlands Maintenance Company of the Royal Engineers. The Orkney Islands were strategically important because they surround and protect the area of deep water called Scapa Flow which had been the base of the Royal Navy in the First World War. Early in the Second World War it had been penetrated by German midget submarines with disastrous results. A decision was made to close the Eastern access to Scapa Flow with a series of causeways linking four islands to the Orkney mainland (to the great benefit after 1945 of the island farmers). These causeways were named the Churchill Barrier. A variety of companies from the Royal Engineers were involved. Mine was concerned with erecting or dismantling hutted camps, built of what were known as Nissen huts: the familiar army huts with a round barrel-shaped roof of corrugated steel on a metal frame, usually eleven metres long and five metres wide. We went from erecting camps to dismantling them, but I failed to make a note of the particular date of this particular turning point in the Second World War.

Now much of the labour force in the building of the barriers closing the Eastern approaches to Scapa Flow, and of my camp-dismantling activities, consisted of Italian prisoners-of-war. They had been captured in North Africa and brought to these bleak, treeless islands in the remotest part of Britain. All those I met seemed to come from the rural South or from Naples. They wore dyed British battledress. Their officers (who were never seen on the sites where they were working) wore smart, well-cut uniforms. Their first question when the truck deposited them on a camp site was *"E quando finirà questa guerra?"* Nissen huts were heated with coke-burning stoves, and one of these, fuelled by scrap timber, would be used to boil potatoes and turnips flavoured with leaves from the roadside, as well as to brew a coffee substitute. They were skilled in curing sheep-skins with alum and salt petre, and some were astonishingly adept at gathering scrap aluminium to make cigarette lighters, in order to provide cash to buy, in Orkney's two towns, Stromness and Kirkwall, the things they couldn't improvise. They taught me the words of the sentimental Neapolitan songs that operatic tenors sing as encores, as well as the usual range of obscene and blasphemous expletives.

However, I am obliged to admit that it was not for blasphemy but for faith that the Italians on Orkney became famous. On the tiny island of Lamb Holm, at the end of the first stretch of causeway, prisoners from Camp 60 erected two of those old Nissen huts, end to end, to built a chapel, lined with *trompe-l'oeil* paintwork on plasterwork, and richly decorated. In 1945, its main motivator, Domenico Chicchetti, a house-painter in civilian life, was permitted to stay in Britain for a few weeks to complete his work after the other prisoners were repatriated. He returned several times with his family in the postwar decades, to undertake maintenance work, and when he died in 1999 it was reported that the chapel had 75,000 visitors a year—four times the population of the Orkney Islands.

I was a keen reader of the novels of Ignazio Silone during the war, and reviewed the English version of Carlo Levi's *Christ Stopped at Eboli* in *Freedom* in 1948, and discussed his *Le Parole Sono Pietre* there in 1956 and its English translation there in 1959. Predictably I was attracted by the postwar Neo-Realism of the Italian cinema. I remember meeting Riccardo Aragno, then the London correspondent of *La Stampa*, who remarked that the interesting thing about London was that the poor formed queues in the East End to see bad films about the rich, while the rich formed queues in the West End to see good films about the poor.

In 1946 I listened eagerly to Marie Louise talking about the journey she and Vero made to Italy, when she was reunited with her mother Giovanna Berneri, after almost ten years, during which Giovanna had been imprisoned, first by the French, then by the Germans, and finally by the Italian Fascists. They also met at Naples her partner in starting the journal *Volontà*, Cesare Zaccaria, and in Milan the interesting circle of people from a new generation, Giancarlo and Guiliana De Carlo and Carlo Doglio.

In 1948 I translated (badly) from *Volontà*, Giancarlo's article on housing problems in Italy. One of my readers was an architectural student John Turner, and when Turner, De Carlo, and I first met in Venice in 1952 we discussed the crucial issues of "who provides and who decides?" in housing and planning. I also met Doglio and Ugo Fedeli, as well as the architect Ludovico Quaroni and others involved in the rehousing of the cave-dwellers of Matera in Lucania described by Carlo Levi. In Naples I met Giovanna and Cesare, and went with them to the children's colony at Sorrento, named in memory of Marie Louise.

Astonishingly I wasn't to visit Italy again until the great international anarchist gathering in Venice in 1984, when Harriet, my partner, and I travelled with Philip Sansom and also David Koven, one of the veterans of the journals *Why?* and *Resistance* in New York. We had of course been visited in England by our less insular friends from Milan, and we count them among our dearest friends.

You are right that I do feel a great empathy with some aspects of Italian life. One is in attitudes to children. My old friend Joe Benjamin, who was the pioneer of "adventure playgrounds" in Britain, used to say, "Children are a modern invention. They used to be part of the family." You will know of the English novelist Tim Parks, long resident in Verona. He wrote a book, *An Italian Education*, comparing Italian and British childhoods. His conclusion is that "I do believe that kids have a better time here, and that adolescence is more fun (in Italy). Certainly I never saw a group of people so confident and at ease themselves and their youth." He could have added that in the Anglo-Saxon countries, adolescents are seen as a *threat* to the adult world.

Another aspect of Italy which I find attractive by comparison with the collapse of manufacturing industry in Britain, that accelerated so disastrously after 1980, is the small-workshop economy that we can observe in regions like Emilia-Romagna, which I had the opportunity to examine in 1988 and described in the course of my book *Welcome, Thinner City*.

These two aspects of Italian life that attract me were brought together by my friend Paul Thompson the historian.

*I know him well. He tutored me for a term at Oxford.*

So you will know his interest both in oral history and in the legacy of William Morris. In his lecture to the William Morris Society in 1991 on *Human Creativity and the Future World Environment*, he described the international comparison he was looking at, involving working lives and family lives in Coventry in England and Turin in Italy, two cities which had both experienced the collapse of the giant factory economy, which was once the model and the archetype of the mass-production industry of the last century:

. . . I found that while the English city in the face
of that crisis seemed depressed and hopeless, the
Italian city was unexpectedly optimistic, indeed
booming with new firms, at all social levels from
engineering design to metal workshops and squatters' vegetable market allotments. Again I have
been struck by apparent links between that inventive adaptability and the ways in which people are
brought up in the two cities. In Coventry—perhaps
as a result of more than three generations of factory work in Britain—interviews brought a picture
of a very rigid type of socialisation. In many families, children were still expected to be seen and not
heard, for example at mealtimes, and indeed some
are expected scarcely to talk or discuss at all with
their parents. Parents seemed surprisingly unable to transmit either their ideas or their hopes or
their skills to them and children were often harshly
disciplined. In Turin, by contrast, children were
brought up with a much more open expression of
affection, and a rare use of physical punishment,
while discussion at table was absolutely central to
family life . . . The case of Turin is not unique: a
similar economic development is found even more
strikingly in Emilia-Romagna, where the remarkable contemporary prosperity of the region is based
extensively on co-operatives . . . Such a democratic
manufacturing economy has no parallel in this
country.

*Your own conception of anarchism was surely very differ-
ent from that of the rest of the Freedom Press Group. How
did you come to develop it? Did your way of seeing things
cause any problems within the Group?*

We all have characteristic ways of thinking. My mode of thinking has its limitations and its advantages. I tend to think in terms of practical examples or actual experiences rather than in theories or hypotheses. This has its useful aspects, but it also means that there is a whole range of theoretical literature that I find too tedious to read. Another aspect of the way I think, and in spite of what I have just said, is that, although I have no background in sociology, my way of looking at most things is a sociological approach. I am especially interested, that is to say, in the *sociology* of music, or politics, or childhood. My knowledge of the sociology of autonomous groups would tell me that it is always more sensible and conducive to the effectiveness of such groups to stress the large areas of agreement, rather than those of differing propaganda emphases.

Two big influences on me in the 1950s were Martin Buber's essay "Society and the State" published in English in 1951 and Alexander Herzen's *From the Other Shore* published in English in 1956. Other influences were the American anarchist propagandists Paul Goodman and David Wieck who related anarchism to ordinary decisions of daily life, in such journals as *Resistance* and *Liberation* and, earlier, *Politics*.

Speculating about "The Unwritten Handbook" in *Freedom* for 28 June 1958, I wrote that

> To my mind the most striking feature of the unwritten handbook of twentieth century anarchism is not its rejection of the insights of the classical anarchist thinkers, Godwin, Proudhon, Bakunin, Kropotkin, but its widening and deepening of them. But it is selective, it rejects perfectionism, utopian fantasy, conspiratorial romanticism, revolutionary

optimism; it draws from the classical anarchists their most valid, not their most questionable ideas. And it adds to them the subtler contribution of later (and neglected because untranslated) thinkers like Landauer and Malatesta. It also adds the evidence provided in this century by the social sciences, by psychology and anthropology, and by technical change.

It is still an anarchism of present and permanent protest—how could it be anything else in our present peril? But it is one which recognises that the choice between libertarian and authoritarian solutions occurs every day and in every way. And the extent to which we choose, or accept, or are fobbed off with, or lack the imagination and inventiveness to discover alternatives to, authoritarian solutions to small problems is the extent to which we are their powerless victims in big affairs. We are powerless to change the course of events over the nuclear arms race, imperialism and so on, precisely because we have surrendered our power over everything else . . .

I don't think my fellow members of the Freedom Press Group would have found this opinion objectionable from an anarchist point of view.

*I never knew this article on "The Unwritten Handbook." What you quote is remarkable and magnificent. Besides the names you mention I also discern the influence of Alex Comfort.*

You are quite right. However, editors are always at the mercy of authors. When I was given the opportunity to start the journal *Anarchy*, the first writer I approached to contribute to the first issue was Comfort. I visited him in his underground room at University College in London, and told him how important his ideas were for me. We laughed about many absurdities of life in 1960, but when his article arrived it was about sex-and-violence in contemporary fiction, witty and perceptive, but not what I really needed to launch a new anarchist journal.

*Anarchy is conventionally—and correctly—judged as one of the best anarchist periodicals to have been published anywhere. How did it come about?*

What you say is very kind, but I think it might be more true to say that various anarchist journals of the past have been the right response to a particular period and social climate. We might say that of *Les Temps Nouveaux* in its particular time in France, or the *Revista Blanca* in its day in Spain. In retrospect, the 1960s were a propitious period for an anarchist journal. The late '50s and the '60s were the years of the struggle against colonialism, of the Hungarian revolution and its suppression by Soviet tanks, of the Anglo-French invasion of Suez, of the Campaign for Nuclear Disarmament and its more radical off-shoots, and of the student revolts. The new movements for women's liberation and homosexual liberation were to come later, in the early '70s. The journal came into existence because I had been arguing, both in *Freedom* and at meetings of the Freedom Press Group, for a monthly, rather than a weekly journal. I cited a number of weekly journals which had ceased publication in Britain in the 1950s and the fact that "serious" political weeklies (for example, the *Spectator* and the *New Statesman*) survived on much reduced circulations. There had on the other hand been an increase in the number of monthly journals. A study had been made of "the anarchist personality" by the psychologist, Tony Gibson, who found that *Freedom*'s readers could be described as "highly-literate people, who think."

I argued (in *Freedom* for 10 December 1960) that weekly publication brought severe disadvantages for the people who produced it.

> So much of their efforts are absorbed by the sheer mechanical task of doing this each week that there is no time to be selective about its contents, no time to make them up into an attractive whole, no time to write to and talk to potential contributors, no time to follow up particular topics dealt with in the paper with people outside our movement who are interested in them, no time to advertise particular issues (of the paper) in the right places, no time for assembling first-rate anarchist reportage, no time for all the vital activities which would make the most of the good material that the paper contains, no time to prune it of stale old clichés and prefabricated phrases, no time to discuss seriously the problems of anarchism.

I urged that "if we are ever to effect the transition from a sect to a social force we need a revitalised *Freedom*," and that it was "Because we have failed to formulate anarchist alternatives in the most prosaic as well as the most important fields of life, that the very people who could bring life to our own activities cannot bring themselves to take us seriously" (*Freedom* 3 December 1960). I produced "mock-up" or dummy versions of my proposals to show what I believed such a journal would look like. My colleagues in the Freedom Press Group responded with a quite reckless open-mindedness and said, in effect, let those who want to produce a weekly do so, and let those who want to produce a monthly do so too. It was decided that in the first week of every month the monthly journal should appear instead of the weekly, and that it should have, not the quarto (A4) format that I envisaged for a monthly *Freedom*, but an octavo (A5) page. I now think this was a good idea, simply because even today I visit people and they pull copies out of their bookshelves preserved precisely because they would fit on a bookshelf.

Faced with the unexpected need to find a title, I selected *Autonomy*, with the subtitle "a journal of anarchist ideas." This had been the title of one of the very first anarchist journals published in Britain. Pressure was put on me to change the title to *Anarchy*, which made the subtitle rather superfluous, though it was retained until the 27th issue, after which it seems to have been dropped by the cover designer, Rufus Segar, rather than by me. I had envisaged a monthly *Freedom*. The dummy versions I handed round at our meeting looked like Dwight Macdonald's *Politics*. But in fact I found myself producing an entirely different journal of which I was the sole editor. It was a remarkably privileged situation. For once the original decisions had been made, I was given an absolute autonomy. Nobody questioned what went into *Anarchy*. Other people in the group undertook the tasks of dealing with subscriptions, bulk order, stamping, and dispatching.

*How would you depict its character? Was* Anarchy's *success to be explained solely in terms of its character—or were there other factors? Of what aspects of the journal are you most proud?*

I think that the important characteristic of *Anarchy* was that it assumed that anarchism was an aspect of every aspect of life and for that reason had to be taken seriously. This is why *The Times* commented that "*Anarchy*'s existence has been nothing if not intellectually adventurous," and why the writer Colin MacInnes, who always did his best to publicize it in the non-anarchist press, kindly wrote that it was "the most original monthly that I know of in its perceptions of shifting trends in our society." The policy of devoting an issue to a particular topic meant that the specialist press in a variety of fields—from physical education to industrial management—were obliged to draw their readers' attention to it.

There were other factors. One was the character of the 1960s that we have already discussed. Another was precisely that the magazine *was* new, and not weighed down with a past. Yet another was the visual excitement of its covers.

I am most proud of the fact that it obliged people to take anarchist ideas seriously, and not dismiss them as the characteristics of a "lunatic fringe" or sect. This was also true of outside contributors who I had persuaded to write for the journal, who found as a result that their personal experience and expertise fitted into a coherent pattern of responding to the world.

*Who are you thinking of? The radical criminologists?*

Yes, among others. As an outsider, invited to talk at universities and polytechnics for the first time, I was shocked by the glib, automatic Marxism that shaped attitudes for both teachers and students. I think that for plenty of them anarchism was a liberating ideology.

*Are there any aspects of* Anarchy *which you came to regret?*

I had several regrets. The first, of course, is that the circulation failed to rise from 2,000 to 4,000 that I aimed at. The second is concerned with themes that *Anarchy* had failed to discuss. After the hundredth issue I was asked to write in *Freedom* (14 June 1969) about the experience. I explained that

> I am convinced that the most effective way of conducting anarchist propaganda through the medium of a monthly journal is to take the whole range of partial, fragmentary, but immediate issues in which people *are actually likely to get involved*, and to seek out anarchist solutions, rather than to indulge in windy rhetoric about revolution. A goal that is infinitely remote, said Alexander Herzen, is not a goal at all, but a deception. On the other hand, these preoccupations lead to a neglect of a whole range of topics which *Anarchy* has ignored. Where, for example, is a thorough anarchist analysis of economic and industrial changes in this country? Not in *Anarchy*, I'm afraid.

*Why did* Anarchy *only last ten years? How did it come to an end? Did the sheer hard work of editing* Anarchy *help or impede your own writing and the generation of your own ideas?*

In May 1970 I notified the other members of the Freedom Group that I was intending to give up editing *Anarchy* at the end of the year. One of the people working at the Freedom Bookshop was eager to take over the editorship from January 1971 and this was agreed. The new series began to appear from Freedom Press, and then severed the connection and then appeared very irregularly.

I had explained that "Ten years is long enough for any but the most exceptional of editors to bring out any journal. Routine and ready-made formulas begin to intrude." I certainly felt this to be true. With the policy of building issues of the journal around specific topics, if someone had failed to produce his or her text on time, in order not to delay publication I would certainly have to write the article myself under a pseudonym. The 1960s were the most eventful decade of my personal life. I changed my occupation from architecture to teaching, and in the course of this had met my partner Harriet, who had been widowed with two small children. I had already become the guardian of two orphaned boys and by the end of the decade Harriet and I had another of our own.

I was very relieved to have withdrawn from *Anarchy* because in December 1970 an advertisement appeared in the *Times Educational Supplement* for the job at the Town and Country Planning Association (a very old voluntary organisation) of starting a journal for teachers, propagating environmental education. I was given the job and called the journal *BEE*, the acronym for *Bulletin of Environmental Education*.

People would tease by saying that I imagined I was still editing *Anarchy*, but the important thing was that the new journal was produced in my employer's time.

I often reflect on how much simpler it would be to produce a journal like *Anarchy* today, after the revolution in printing. It was left to the cover designer, Rufus Segar to describe, in a late issue, the process of production, which was a tour of inner London and its suburbs:

> The way the magazine is put together is comic, awful, and, for a journal of dissent, too vulnerable. The words are assembled by the editor and sent to a trade typesetters in Stepney. The proofs are

made up into a dummy in Putney. The metal type
for titles is made up in Whitechapel. The picture for
the cover is made in St. James's and sent to a block-
maker in Clerkenwell. The block is sent to a printer
in Bishopsgate who prints the covers. The insides
and the covers are collected together and taken to a
binders in Fulham who folds the insides, stitches on
the covers and trims the copies. The magazines are
sent to Whitechapel for dispatch. Sometimes you
get your magazine late. The process is Victorian . . .

Rufus failed to mention one step in the process, that of
proof-reading. Contrary to the rumour spread by my dear
friend Nicolas Walter, the proofs were read, but there was
no method of checking on the insertion of corrected lines.
And on just one occasion (no. 35, January 1964) the cor-
rections were not inserted at all!

There was even one occasion when the main author,
Robert Ollendorf, boycotted Rufus Segar's cover for an issue on Wilhelm Reich, regarding it as frivolous, while the
binders boycotted it claiming it was obscene. On another
occasion the cover design failed to arrive in time for the
printer, so that I had to provide an instant handwritten
cover for an issue on the fishing industry.

My life as a writer of books did not begin until after
my editing of *Anarchy* (there was never any time to consider a book) but it was certainly helped by that experience. Several books of mine in the 1970s were the direct
result of approaches from publishers as a result of their
having read articles I had written there in the 1960s.

*And your own ideas and conception of anarchism? Did the
decade of* Anarchy *help to develop them? Or were they, as
it seems, fully formed by the end of the 1950s?*

Like most people in most aspects of life I probably would not consciously observe changes in my opinions. What *did* happen, as a result of readers in many fields of life, reading an anarchist argument, by chance, is that they responded in two different ways. One was to say, "Well, if anarchism is the belief that you have described, I have always been an anarchist without knowing it." The other was to say, "The way writers in *Anarchy* have depicted the 'gang system' of self-organised workers in manufacturing industry, or the way that small, family firms of lorry drivers would share out journeys between them, reminds me of the 'organised chaos' or 'anarchy' of the place where I work." They were people who discovered that, as I always claimed, anarchy is a theory of organisation.

All these encounters broadened my approach to anarchist propaganda.

*For most of your life you have been involved with architecture, housing, and planning. How did that come about?*

I mentioned that when I was sixteen I went to work for an architect whose own early influences were members of the Arts and Crafts movement. They included people he met a century ago at the Central School of Arts and Crafts in London, like Edward Johnson and Eric Gill, and especially that school's principal, the architectural philosopher W.R. Lethaby. When I finally got out of the army, I returned to his office but soon moved to more typical architectural and planning practices. They included, firstly the Architects' Co-partnership, and then for ten years, the firm of Shepheard and Epstein, and finally Chamberlin, Powell, and Bon, which I left (as Director of Research) in 1964.

Any reader familiar with the architectural world will recognize that those London practices of the postwar decades had completely different design ideologies, but had several common characteristics. They were all private firms engaged on large public buildings. Their work in the 1950s and 1960s was mostly housing, schools, and health buildings for public authorities. That generation of architects was nurtured by, and employed by, the welfare state. They shared it social ideology, but also of course, its paternalistic assumptions.

*And as for those design ideologies? How did they vary from practice to practice?*

The Architects' Co-partnership was a team of young left-wing people, working in the mainstream of the modern movement. Their most famous building was the Brynmawr rubber factory, built to provide alternative employment in the very depressed mining area of South Wales. It had a spectacular series of reinforced concrete domes, but did not succeed in its social purpose. Peter Shepheard's design aim was to building modest, simple buildings which would "grow old gracefully" unlike so many postwar buildings. Chamberlin, Powell, and Bon had a far more assertive view of the function of the designer. I'm sure you're familiar with their work at Leeds University and at New Hall, Cambridge. Their most famous work was the vast Barbican complex in the City of London, an example of what, I suppose, has to be called the new monumentality.

In contrast to the actual buildings that resulted from three different approaches to modern architecture, one question seldom raised, when less self-assertive architects are concerned, is that of the social role of architects in the fields of housing and schools. A friend of mine, the architect Steve Musgrave, examined the extent to which design decisions in housing were made by either architects or building users, and found that "Instead of meeting his clients face to face, getting to understand clients' needs and preferences . . . these are mediated by other departments and by the central government, all of whom are equally innocent of any systematic contact with tenants." It became evident to me very early that from an anarchist point of view, dweller control is the first principle of housing.

*Please tell me about your working life: in architects' offices, as a further education teacher and as education officer for the Town and Country Planning Association.*

Our mutual friend Vernon Richards—the man who revived anarchist publishing in Britain in 1936—used to say until his death in 2001 that one of the books he hoped to write was about *A Working Life*. It would, he often told me in his last year, begin with an account of his childhood in Soho, where he had the freedom of the street from infancy, and would then describe his life as a civil engineer (he had a degree in engineering) which ended when the editors of *Freedom* were arrested in 1945, and when he was sentenced to nine months in prison. He resolved while in prison that there was no sense in pursuing a career as an engineer, and his unwritten book would have described his subsequent adventures in earning a livelihood as a grocer (running the business of his mother's grocery shop, King Bomba), as a photographer (several books of his photographs were eventually published by Freedom Press in the 1990s), as a travel courier accompanying visitors to Franco's Spain and Brezhnev's Soviet Union (he believed that holiday travel would open closed frontiers), and as a grower of organic vegetables on a one-hectare site for over twenty years until he reached the age of eighty-two. He was also, in those twenty years, the deliverer of Sunday newspapers over a wide rural area. This enabled him to read the entire press, to find a market for his vegetables and to meet the costs of keeping a car.

All these occupations were, of course, subservient to his really important preoccupations: those of an anarchist editor, writer, and publisher. I have argued with him that most of us are not skillful enough or versatile enough to embrace such a variety of occupations and remain solvent, but in retrospect, I too have made some big shifts in work, with some well-timed changes of livelihood.

I have told you how I drifted into the world of architecture when a boy, in a way that would be impossible today when training is dominated by the schools of architecture and professional qualifications. I enjoyed that atmosphere of the drawing-offices where I worked in 1950s, libertarian and non-hierarchical. People who were my employers then have been dear friends ever since. Our work in those days was on public housing and schools, and I became aware of big changes in the ideology of education.

By the 1960s, just as architecture was losing its glamour, and just as the commissions for architects were becoming office blocks rather than schools and housing, and when I was editing *Anarchy* in my spare time, I was hoping to make a shift into teaching. I was not eligible for training as a teacher because I had left school at fifteen with no qualifications, and I could not contemplate poverty as a student for more than one year. However, one avenue was open to me: that of a one-year course to qualify for someone like me, with years of technical employment, as a teacher in what in Britain is called "further education."

In Britain we have primary schools for ages five to eleven, secondary schools for ages eleven to sixteen or eighteen, and, below university level, Further Education Colleges, which at that time had a preponderance of young workers who came to the college one day a week on "day-release." This was a very attractive part of the education machine, where young people who had rejected school, found themselves re-valuing education as "students" rather than as "children."

In the early 1960s in Britain, a report on the failings of technical education had concluded that technical training was too narrow and should be liberalized. But the official decision was a typical bureaucratic compromise. Some of Kropotkin's most interesting pages, both in his autobiography and in his *Fields, Factories and Workshops*, were precisely about the liberalization of technical training. (See Michael P. Smith: *The Libertarian and Education,* Allen & Unwin, 1983). But the official decision was that instead of a broader approach, a new, and of course compulsory, subject should be added to the curriculum, and called Liberal Studies. Its content was determined by the teacher.

My one-year teacher-training course at Garnett College in South London in 1964–65 was enjoyable, partly because I had left school so many years earlier in 1939, but mostly because Harriet, a fellow student, has been my partner ever since.

After our year at Garnett College, she moved on to Kingsway Day College, a famous experimental college in central London, where she taught history, and I moved first to Croydon Technical College and then to Wandsworth Technical College in South London, where I was in charge of Liberal Studies and, since the college was unwilling to appoint enough permanent staff to cover this suspect topic, I would engage a variety of remarkably interesting people to undertake part-time teaching.

My own teaching was determined by the expressed needs of these young electrical or mechanical engineering apprentices, and the areas of life they felt they knew too little about. As you can imagine, these were such topics as sexual relations, safe drinking, the police and their rights, and so on. Exactly like anybody else, meeting young workers at that time, I was surprised by the lack of ordinary information my students had acquired after ten years of compulsory schooling, and how unprepared for the adult world they were.

But other teachers were far more adventurous. We heard of bold initiatives at Ipswich Civic College, and of an explosion of new writers among the day-release students at Yeovil Technical College in the West of England, while Albert Hunt's students restaged the Russian Revolution in the streets of Bradford. The unregulated freedom of the teachers in this very small proportion of the time of part-time students was too good to be permanent, and by 1970 there was a move to impose a curriculum and to change the name of the subject itself from Liberal Studies to "communication studies" or "technical writing."

But then, as I explained to you, the Town and Country Planning Association (TCPA) advertised for an Environmental Education Officer whose task would be to provide a service for school-teachers who were anxious to introduce environmental issues into their teaching, by means of a monthly journal. Anthony Fyson was appointed as my assistant because, like me, he had a background of both architecture and planning, and of teaching. We dispatched the first issue of our *Bulletin of Environmental Education* to every school in Britain. By good luck, it was well-timed. The arguments about an environmental crisis and a way out of it, which were put forward by the editors of the *Ecologist* in their book *A Blueprint for Survival* (Penguin, 1972), were dismissed as alarmist, until in the same year a vast increase in oil prices brought a global recession and a new concern about our profligacy with resources and our dependency on fossil fuels.

We spent the 1970s travelling around schools and talking to teachers and children, while circulating their experiences in *BEE*. But this was expensive and Anthony Fyson and I had to seek out consultancy tasks in order to enable our employers to pay our salaries. One of the most interesting of these was a project called Art and the Built Environment, in which I was concerned with Eileen Adams, a brilliant art teacher, in exploring the role of art, both as a school subject and as a human activity, in our understanding of the environment.

I remember the 1970s as wonderfully creative years, which are reflected in the book by Eileen and me (Adams and Ward, *Art and the Built Environment*, Longmans, 1982), in my book *Talking Schools* (Freedom Press, 1995) and in my article "Education for Mastery of the Environment" which Giancarlo De Carlo published in *Spazio e Società* (no. 4, December 1978).

Obviously, publishing a journal aimed at teachers, we would meet the most busy and environmentally enthusiastic of them, but I was immensely impressed by the people I met in my education years, and the exploration of the local environment that they inspired from their children.

*What led you to take the plunge to become a full-time writer? Have you ever regretted it?*

There are several reasons. One was the ordinary domestic one that Harriet and I hoped to move from the city to the country, where we hoped that life would be less expensive, and the summer of 1980 was the best time to make this move because our elder boys had completed their secondary schooling while the youngest was about to make the transition from primary to secondary school. Another was that the financial position of TCPA was very insecure at that time, and yet another was that I would never find such an enjoyable job again. I strongly agree with the findings of some industrial psychologists that satisfaction in work is strongly related to the "span of autonomy," by which is meant the extent of a worker's time in which he or she is free to make his/her own decisions. I see this as an important measure of both pleasure and fulfilment in work. I had a greater than usual span of autonomy in almost all of my working life, and most of all when I was employed by the TCPA. Ever since I stopped working there in 1979, I have written a monthly column in the TCPA journal, *Town and Country Planning*. It is called "People and Ideas" which was the title given to my weekly column in *Freedom* in the 1950s.

It was also important that in the previous decade, I had, at last, the time to produce books. My output seemed phenomenal only because this was a late beginning (I was aged forty-six in 1970) and there were so many books waiting to be compiled. My first two little books *Violence* (1970) and *Work* (1972) were excitingly illustrated school books intended for reluctant readers aged fourteen to sixteen, in a series edited by Richard Mabey for Penguin Education. They were used in much wider ways and were reprinted continually all through the 1970s. Ever since then I have met people who read them at school. Penguin Education was a very innovative subsidiary of Penguin Books, and *Utopia* (1974) was written for their "Human Space" series, intended to transform the teaching of geography for children aged eleven to fourteen. But no sooner was it published, when the ownership of Penguin Books changed, and the new controllers closed the Education department. So I acquired about 2,000 copies of the books and gave a parcel to every school I visited.

*Anarchy in Action* (1973), was, as you know, the result of my editing *Anarchy* and is a kind of manual of anarchist applications. The book I wrote with Anthony Fyson, *Streetwork: The Exploding School* (1973), described the ideas on environmental education that he and I were propagating through *BEE*. I was asked to edit the book *Vandalism* (1973) as a result of the issue of *Anarchy* on "Creative Vandalism" that I had produced in 1966, and the book *Tenants Take Over* (1974) was written as a result of my article with that title in *Anarchy* in 1968. The ensuing publicity led to a request for a book of my articles and lectures on housing for Freedom Press, *Housing: An Anarchist Approach* (1976). Meanwhile other publishers had asked me to edit new editions of Kropotkin's *Fields, Factories and Workshops* (1974) and his *Memoirs of a Revolutionist* (1978). My final book of the 1970s was *The Child in the City* (1978), a book which still follows me around. An Italian version appeared as recently as 2000.

All these books were produced when I still had full-time employment, so you can understand that, since there are so many hours in a day, I had to become a full-time writer. Predictably I have had a very low income since I made that decision, but I have not regretted it.

*I have never understood the connection you see between planning and anarchism. Isn't planning authoritarian and controlled? Aren't "new towns" more compatible with state rather than libertarian socialism? Would you please explain?*

For most of us in Britain, town and country planning
is a branch of local government determining that whatever you want to do with a piece of land or an existing
building, you have to have planning permission (and
pay a large fee for your application). It is governed by
21 Acts of Parliament, 223 Statutory Instruments, and
over 1,000 pages of official policy indications which must
be taken into account when any application is considered. Central government indicates its policy by allowing
or refusing appeals against local government decisions.
Only the persistent and the rich appeal, and they make
fortunes for lawyers. The whole system is corrupt, not
through bribery, but because it favours rich developers
and penalizes the poor, who are invariably the *victims*
of planning.

The tragedy of the corruption of planning is that it is
sensible for human communities, urban or rural to plan
their future use of land. And it is important to stress that
in Britain, after the publication of Ebenezer Howard's
*Garden Cities of Tomorrow* a century ago, planning was
seen as a popular crusade, not as a branch of government. Peter Hall, our best-known historian of planning,
goes further. In his book *Cities of Tomorrow* (Oxford:
Blackwell, 1988), which has the subtitle "An intellectual
history of urban planning and design in the twentieth
century," he examines a series of visions of the future of
the urban environment and their impact on what actually
happened. On page three of his book, under the heading
"The Anarchist Roots of the Planning Movement," Hall
explains that

> Specifically, the book will argue that in this pro-
> cess of belatedly translating ideal into reality,
> there occurred a rather monstrous perversion of

history. The really striking point is that many, though by no means all, of the early visions of the planning movement stemmed from the anarchist movement which flourished in the last decades of the nineteenth century and the first years of the twentieth. That is true of Howard, of Geddes and of the Regional Planning Association of America, as well as of many derivatives on the mainland of Europe. (To be sure, it was very definitely untrue of Le Corbusier, who was an authoritarian centralist, and of most members of the City Beautiful movement, who were faithful servants of finance capitalism or of totalitarian dictators.) The vision of these anarchist pioneers was not merely an alternative built form, but of an alternative society, neither capitalist nor bureaucratic-socialistic: a society based on voluntary co-operation among men and women, working and living in small self-governing commonwealths.

Peter Hall similarly stressed the anarchist implications of popular intervention in housing and planning in a lecture in Amsterdam and in the address he was invited to give to the 75th anniversary conference of the Royal Town Planning Institute in November 1989, where he chose to stress that

> . . . there has been a very general groundswell in the last five years in favour of what could be called the neo-anarchist tradition of planning: the tradition that goes directly back to Patrick Geddes and Ebenezer Howard, and behind them to their spiritual fathers, Peter Kropotkin and Michael Bakunin and Pierre-Joseph Proudhon.

*I wasn't aware that Howard, in particular, was in any way connected to the anarchist movement. Was he really?*

No, but he and Kropotkin praised each other's work and had probably attended each other's lectures. Howard had no belief in the state and his garden cities were conceived as self-organising welfare societies. However, when I was asked to comment in *Freedom* on the influence that Peter Hall generously attributed to John Turner and to me, I remarked that "If you put your hands into what actually happens in the planning and housing scene, they are bound to get dirty with every kind of compromise."

And you are quite correct in seeing the British New Towns as more compatible with state, rather than libertarian, socialism. The two Garden Cities that Howard actually initiated were pathetically under-funded, and the New Towns in Britain funded by government after the Second World War were far from his ideal. I always defend them, as in my book *New Town, Home Town* (1993), because they were more successful than the series of disastrous government policies for inner cities or for municipal development on the urban fringe. They were the one opportunity for inner-city working-class families to join the exodus from our grossly overcrowded cities that Howard correctly prophesied. This is the reason for the snobbish disdain for the British New Towns that you often discern among people who would never dream of visiting any of them.

However, I agree with your view that the defects of the British New Town program relate precisely to paternalist state socialism, and within the New Town world I am notorious as an advocate of a more "anarchist" approach, not as an apologist for state socialism. Thus, in his history of the TCPA, Dennis Hardy explains that

Colin Ward was to play a key role in the early stages of the "revivalist" movement, and if there is a single date to mark the start of it all it is that of his presentation of an imaginative paper, "The Do-it-yourself New Town" at a conference in 1975. In this, Ward argued for a new concept of building communities, in which the residents themselves would be involved directly in planning, designing and building their own homes and neighbourhoods. The role of local authorities would be limited to that of site provision and basic services. His ideas were formed against a background of sensing that while the official new towns programme was running out of steam, at the same time there was evidence of a lively "alternatives" movement in which self-reliance was an important feature.

Over the coming year or so, Ward's proposal, through exposure in various publications and at events (such as that to celebrate the seventy-fifth anniversary of the formation of Letchworth) gradually gained wider support.[2]

*So this isn't at odds with the importance you have attributed, since as far back as the 1940s, to squatting?*

No. In Britain, contrary to the way it is presented by government and the popular press, squatting is almost invariably the occupation by homeless people of publicly owned housing which has been empty for a considerable time. So I have supported squatting in empty property in New Towns as much as in old cities. I think squatters' campaigns, as

2    *From New Towns to Green Politics: Campaigning for Town and Country Planning, 1946–1990* (London: E & FN Spon, 1991), p. 173.

well as providing a roof for homeless people, are significant as a symbolic challenge to the concept of property, and for their effect on the participants. As I said in the book *Anarchy in Action*, it "reveals a great deal about the state of mind that is induced by free and independent action, and that which is induced by dependence and inertia: the difference between people who initiate things and act for themselves and people to whom things just happen."

*How does this relate to dweller control, which you have mentioned earlier and which time and again you emphasise as an essential feature of a free society?*

I see dweller control as the ideal in the universal need for housing, just as I see workers' control as the ideal in industry. It is also far more easy to achieve. Different countries have evolved different forms of housing tenure. In Britain in 1914, 90 percent of households, rich or poor, rented their homes from a private landlord, and about nine percent of households were owner-occupied. By 1974 only about 14 percent rented their homes from private landlords, and 53 percent were owner-occupiers, while 33 percent rented from local authorities.

By the year 2000 the percentage of homes rented from local authorities had been reduced by government policies initiated by Mrs. Thatcher and continued by the Labour government. Owner-occupation had become 68 percent.

In the Scandinavian countries a large proportion of households belonged to housing co-operatives. In spite of Britain being seen as the home of the co-operative movement, when I wrote my book *Tenants Take Over* in 1974 there were only two or three housing co-ops in the whole country. Today there are about a thousand: still a pathetically small number.

The book *Tenants Take Over* argued that municipal housing was in crisis because of three factors: remote and paternalistic management, the neglect of maintenance, and the culture of enforced dependency. It argued that ownership and management should be transferred to tenant cooperatives. As a result of the book I was asked to address innumerable meetings of tenants and of housing committee members. The book had a salutary effect in Liverpool during a brief period when the Liberals controlled the city's housing policy. It inspired several instances, not of the transfer of control of existing housing to tenants, but of newly built housing where the tenants of old, slum houses were enabled to find a site, and commission an architect to design their own new housing. The Hesketh Street Co-op and the Weller Streets Co-op, succeeded in a very poor part of the city. The proudest moment of my housing advocacy was when the Weller Streets Co-op chairman, Billy Floyd, introduced me at a meeting by waving a tattered copy of *Tenants Take Over* and saying, "Here's the man who wrote the Old Testament . . . but we *built* the New Jerusalem!"

Among politicians, the Labour Party denied that there was a crisis of housing management and maintenance, while Conservatives read the book with interest. Liberals supported my argument. When Mrs. Thatcher came to power the main plank of her housing policy was the sale at a discount of municipal housing to the individual tenants who occupied it. My book had a chapter called "One by one, or all together?" anticipating this.

*Does this mean that you are a supporter of the privatization of municipal housing?*

I would argue that the transfer of council-owned housing to its occupants is the best guarantee of its survival.

Everyone knows of the sad decline into obsolescence of public housing. Councils blame government restrictions on their expenditure. More thoughtful people reflect that public housing is the only sector of the market in which houses have a limited life. Owner-occupied housing goes on for ever. It is improved, extended, and updated by one generation after another. Dweller control of housing, whether individual or collective, ensures that the enormous investment in housing in the past is rescued rather than wasted.

I am endlessly quoting the message that John Turner brought back from his experiences in Latin America, which I describe as Turner's First Law of Housing:

> When dwellers control the major decisions and are free to make their own contribution to the design, construction or management of their housing, both the process and the environment produced stimulate individual and social well-being. When people have no control over, nor responsibility for key decisions in the housing process, on the other hand, dwelling environments may instead become a barrier to personal fulfilment and a burden on the economy.

I think that if we modified this statement to apply to other important aspects of life, for example, work or education, we would have achieved a definition of anarchism.

*Yes, I agree. It was William Hague, who as a schoolboy speaker at a Conservative Party conference famously called for "the rolling back of the frontiers of the state." I imagine that most anarchists responded to this slogan with some sympathy; but how have you reacted to the Conservative governments' implementation of the denationalization of gas, electricity, and water, as well as of coal, steel, and the railways?*

I don't believe that many anarchists would be excited by the so-called Libertarianism of the political Right, or would see it as anything but the worship of the market economy. Before the nationalization program of the post-war Labour government, gas and electricity were mostly municipal enterprises and were a source of revenue to local authorities and thus a useful area of local autonomy. Coal, steel, and the railways were bankrupt industries when nationalized by the Labour government, and public control had been thought necessary to provide the modernization neglected by private capitalist owners. Mrs. Thatcher's government presided over the virtual extinction of the coal and steel industries, condemned because they were not profitable. The sale of Britain's water supplies to private speculators was a disgrace described in detail in the first chapter of my book *Reflected in Water* (London: Cassell, 1997). The sale of the railway system has made Britain's railways the least reliable in Europe.

In practice, the Conservative governments of the 1980s and 1990s in Britain pushed forward the frontiers of the state in many respects. They greatly reduced the income and freedom of action of local authorities; they circumscribed the autonomy of teachers and schools, which, for the first time in their history, were obliged to adhere to a National Curriculum. Their penal policy and their attitude to civil liberties were heavily punitive and prescriptive.

*That, without doubt, is the case. But I have been wanting to ask you about right-wing libertarianism. Do you see it as entirely negative? Or does it have any positive features?*

Most of the right-wing libertarians that I have read about in the press, or heard on the radio, seem to have failed to notice that we live in a class-divided society where opportunities in life are immensely unequal. However, I must add that in 1995 I met David Green of the Institute of Economic Affairs (which is seen as a right-wing libertarian think-tank), I found that he was a critic, not a defender, of Thatcherism, and was, of course, like me, a critic too of the automatic assumptions of the political Left and of its faith in the state.

*Now the Labour governments of Tony Blair are pressing ahead with part-privatization or public-private schemes: in London Transport, the National Health Service, even the schools. How do you envisage an anarchist society organizing transport?*

I have certainly been disturbed by the ultimate triumphs of the Thatcher ideology. How she must be smiling at the way she has won over her Labour Party successors to the religion of market-worship, and has infiltrated everybody's day-to-day language with the jargon of business schools.

I want to see transport managed by the community and the transport workers. In my book *Anarchy in Action*, I cite the effect on railway systems of centralist and decentralist traditions. In Britain and France all the railways are centred on London or Paris. But in Switzerland, the densest railway system in the world serves the smallest localities and the most remote valleys. This is because of the existence of a decentralist political structure and the existence, when the railways were built, of a "democratic railway movement."

*Can you tell me more about the Swiss democratic railway movement?*

Only what I learned many years ago from the architect Christof Bon and from Herbert Luethy who explained that it arose from fierce arguments between small, local communities whose future was dramatically changed by railway access, and who demanded that if they were to pay their share of the cost of bridging and tunnelling in a mountainous country, they should share the benefits, however uneconomic this was for railway builders based in the big cities. In Britain today, we too, need a democratic railway movement. To my mind the nearest approach to this is organized by Paul Salveson of the Transport Research and Information Network (Brian Jackson Centre, New North Parade, Huddersfield HD1 5JP). He looks beyond the current muddle and does not seek a return to the centralized monolith of British Rail. He wants a community-controlled transport system.

*How do you envisage an anarchist society organizing medicine and the health service, and education? Do you see the British welfare state as having possessed any positive features?*

The National Health Service in Britain was instituted in 1948, but of course, long before that, most employed workers (though not their families) had "free" medical treatment through the network of friendly societies that began as organs of working-class self-help in the previous century. Some of these were already providing medical and hospital care for everyone in the district. We could have had a health service directed from below.

In Britain we have an education system funded out of taxation, which includes schools controlled by various religious organizations, as well as a private sector in which affluent parents pay fees. The most useful example of an alternative to the British system (without waiting for the advent of an anarchist society) would be to emulate the Danish system which operates on the assumption, as Robert Powell puts it in his pamphlet on *The Danish Free School Tradition* (Human Scale Education, 96 Carlingcott, near Bath BA2 8AW), "that it is families themselves and not central government, who usually know what is best for their children." Denmark has hundreds of small schools set up by groups of parents and teachers, which receive 75 percent of their funds from the national education budget.

The positive feature of welfare legislation is that, contrary to the capitalist ethic, it is a testament to human solidarity. The negative feature is precisely that it is an arm of the state. I continually find myself quoting the conclusion of Kropotkin in *Modern Science and Anarchism* that "the economic and political liberation of man will have to create new forms for its expression in life, instead of those established by the State" and that "we will be compelled to find new forms of organization for the social functions that the state fulfils through the bureaucracy."

*And what about an anarchist agriculture?*

My guide to an anarchist agriculture has always been Kropotkin's *Fields, Factories and Workshops*, which I had the pleasure of editing for a modern readership. The arguments of his book, over a century ago, were four in number. The first was that there is a trend for manufacturing industry to decentralize throughout the world, and that production for a local market is a rational and desirable tendency. The second was that this implies that each region of the globe should feed itself, and that labor-intensive rather than land-intensive farming could meet the basic needs of a densely populated country like Britain. The third was that the dispersal of industry on a small scale and in combination with agriculture is also rational and desirable, and the fourth was that we need an education which combines manual and intellectual work.

There are trends in the world today that both confirm and contradict Kropotkin's expectations. The global economy results in the supermarkets of Europe being filled with food transported from the ends of the earth, but it remains true that much of the food of the cities of South-East Asia is grown in the city itself. (See *Urban Agriculture: Food, Jobs and Sustainable Cities,* New York: United Nations Development Program, 1996.) Kropotkin's vision is very relevant for the people who are today seeking alternatives to current exploitative approaches.

*Are you a vegetarian?*

Ours is not a vegetarian household ideologically, but has been for long periods in practice, simply because there are plenty of vegetarians in the next generation of our family.

*What view do you take of animal liberation?*

Fifty years ago I knew a Serbian anarchist, Ivan Avakumović who believed that after the liberation of the human race, the period of anarcho-animalism would begin. Current revelations of the ways in which animals are treated by the food-production industry are enough to make animal liberators of us all.

*And what about experiments of animals in the name of medical science?*

All the drugs we use to combat disease or to relieve pain were tested on animals originally and I am sufficiently anthropocentric to prefer that they were not tested on fellow humans. On the other hand I am interested to learn that experiments using animals have been reduced by one half in the last twenty years as a result of propaganda from animal rights campaigners. As always, the zealots have brought discredit on the whole movement by issuing death threats to certain pharmacological researchers, including the leading experimenter in overcoming asthma, a field of medicine of personal interest to me.

But of greater interest is the fact that dirty water is the most common cause of illness throughout the world, while diarrhea is the world's second most serious killer of children, but could easily be prevented or cured.

*Water is something, which unusually for you, you have written about on a global scale.*

Yes, I was very happy to have the opportunity to write a book about water in a series on "Global Issues" (*Reflected in Water: A Crisis of Social Responsibility*, London: Cassell, 1997). You are correct. I have seldom had the chance of writing on an international scale, with the result that when books of mine are translated into other languages, I always feel apologetic for their Anglo-centricity.

In British politics, water was not an industry nationalized by Labour. It had been a Conservative government that replaced a tapestry of small local undertakings with regional water authorities. And when Mrs. Thatcher's government came to power in 1979, nobody anticipated that one of its achievements would be to change the nature of water from a common good to a commodity. One result was that, despite the United Nations resolution that all people have a right of access to water, in 1994 in Britain 12,500 households were disconnected from the water supply because they could not pay their water charges.

The great advantage of being able to discuss the subject on a global scale was that it enabled me to explore the way the building of large dams is linked with the displacement of local populations and the local economy for the benefit of the rich. I was also able to discuss the role of women in the water economy throughout the world, and to describe the way in which export crops are irrigated at the expense of crops for local consumption.

I was particularly glad to discuss from an anarchist standpoint Garrett Hardin's thesis on the "tragedy of the commons" stressing that local popular control is the best way of avoiding it, and that all through history local communities have devised ways of ensuring fair share of a vital and limited resource.

*Would you explain for our readers what is meant by the "tragedy of the commons"?*

Garrett Hardin, Professor of Biology at the University of California, published a paper with this title in 1968 in which he asked us to imagine an ancient common pasture on which every herdsman grazed his animals. It could work reasonably well, he argued, because wars, poaching, and disease kept the numbers of both man and beast well below the carrying capacity of the land. "Finally, however, comes the day when the long-desired goal of social stability becomes a reality. At this point, the inherent logic of the commons remorselessly generates tragedy." The reason for this, he argued is that each herdsman would pursue his own interest by increasing his herd, while the common land will become devastatingly overgrazed.

Needless to say, Hardin's argument was seized upon by advocates of the market economy and by defenders of the gross inequalities involved in private property in land. So in the context of access to water as a scarce resource, I was happy to be able to cite examples from around the world where local communities have ensured fair access. Among them, of course, is the famous *Tribunal de las Aquas* in Valencia, by now a tourist attraction, where farmers meet weekly to apportion water and to settle infringements or disputes over the network of canals, channels, and drains in a vast area.

> No lawyers and none of the state's laws are involved. Proceedings are verbal and are not recorded. Fines are sometimes imposed and are always paid. The tribunal is said to have existed continuously since its foundation by the Moors in 960 AD.

You can see why I regard my book on water as anarchist propaganda.

*I regard* Arcadia for All *as one of your finest achievements, original and sustained. How did this book come about?*

That book was a collaboration with the geographer Dennis Hardy, who had previously written a history of utopian settlements in Britain. It is a study of self-built working-class housing in South-East England, from the years 1900 to 1939 when, during the prolonged agricultural depression, land was sold in small plots to low-income people seeking a holiday home, or week-end retreat, or subsistence chicken-farm. Their development, and the opposition to it, was a fascinating story.

It was a beautiful piece of research, simply because we were able, if we encountered an old survivor, or a cache of old documents, to get on a train and gather every scrap of information. We had the funding to do it well.

*You have co-authored various works, your collaborators including Dennis Hardy, David Crouch, and Peter Hall, as well as the novelist Ruth Rendell. Is this something you enjoy?*

Certainly, these were all happy collaborations. Dennis, David, and Peter are all geographers, and explorations tended to be of popular and unofficial uses of the environment. With Dennis Hardy, I went on to explore the history of the British holiday camp, and with David Crouch, the history and significance of allotment gardens. Peter Hall is our foremost urban geographer, who has recognized the anarchist contribution, so it was a pleasure to work with him on the book *Sociable Cities*, which celebrated the centenary of Ebenezer Howard's book of 1898, *Tomorrow! A Peaceful Path to Real Reform*.

At the height of the Thatcher years, a British publisher approached various well-known writers to produce pamphlets opposing the regime. One was Ruth Rendell, and, living in the village next to ours, she asked me to collaborate on an account of our villages in the coming century, in the pamphlet called *Undermining the Central Line* (London: Chatto & Windus, 1989). What pleased us both was that people assumed that her sections were written by me, and my sections by her. Collaboration has always been a pleasure for me.

*Do you agree that your major intellectual and political debt is to Kropotkin?*

Yes. Kropotkin has so many virtues as an anarchist propagandist. He writes simply, clearly, and logically with the result that his pamphlets and his manual for a revolutionary society, *The Conquest of Bread*, were read aloud and debated by groups of peasants all over Spain and Latin America. *Mutual Aid* is his treatise on social organization, which at the same time served as a refutation of the widespread use of Darwin's theory of Natural Selection to justify competitive capitalist exploitation. And as I explained in my edition of his *Fields, Factories and Workshops*, that remarkable book had several important functions in his system of ideas. Firstly he combatted the idea that there were technical reasons for the tendency of industrial and agricultural organization in modern society to grow larger and larger—a standard objection of anarchist and decentralist ideas. Its second function—as a matter of revolutionary strategy—was to cope with the problem posed by dependence on imported food which implies that a nation in revolt can be starved into submission. Its third function was to advocate the kind of dispersed production for local consumption which is appropriate to the kind of society he wanted, and its final purpose was to deny that the dehumanisation of labour is the price we must pay for a modern industrial society. I am aware of course of Kropotkin's deficiencies. Errico Malatesta described his colleague's "excessive enthusiasm" in a well-known article which at the same time recognized his old friend's immense contribution. It was Malatesta who took care to remind us that we are "only one of the forces acting in society, and history will advance as always, in the direction of the resultant of all the forces." We have therefore, he added, to "find ways of living among non-anarchists as anarchistically as possible."

*What other key influences would you wish to name?*

I mentioned earlier that two other influences on the way that I approach anarchist propaganda were Alexander Herzen and Martin Buber. I was thinking in the first case of Herzen's essay *From the Other Shore* and his criticism of the zealots who accepted the notion, subsequently preached by the Bolsheviks in Russia, and their spokesmen elsewhere, that one generation has to forego its aspirations for the sake of the future. Herzen's response was:

> If progress is the end, for whom are we working? Who is this Moloch who, as the toilers approach him, instead of rewarding them, only recedes, and as a consolation to the exhausted, doomed multitudes crying "We, who are about to die, salute thee," can give back only the mocking answer that after their death all will be beautiful on earth. Do you truly wish to condemn all human beings alive today to the sad role of caryatids supporting a floor for others some day to dance on . . . or of wretched galley slaves, up to their knees in mud, dragging a large barge filled with some mysterious treasure and with the humble words "Progress in the Future" inscribed on its bows? An end that is infinitely remote is not an end, but a trap; an end must be nearer—it ought to be, at the very least, the labourer's wage, or pleasure in the work done. Each age, each generation, each life, had and has its own fullness . . .

Buber was an important influence for me, not only for his book *Paths in Utopia*, about the evolution of libertarian socialism, but especially for his lecture on "Society and the State" given in 1950 at the Hebrew University of Jerusalem where he was Professor of Social Philosophy. He traces through sages from Plato to Bertrand Russell the confusion between the social principle and the political principle. The social principle he sees in families, informal groups, unions, co-operative bodies, and communities, and the political principle in power, authority, dominion, the State. For Buber,

> The fact that every people feels itself threatened by the others gives the State its definitive unifying power; it depends upon the instinct of self-preservation of society itself; the latent external crisis enables it when necessary to get the upper hand in internal crises.

Administration in the sphere of the social principle, says Buber, is equivalent to government in that of the political principle. But

> All forms of government have this in common: each possesses more power than is required by the given conditions; in fact, this excess in the capacity for making dispositions is actually what we understand by political power. The measure of this excess, which cannot of course be computed precisely, represents the exact difference between Administration and Government. I call it the 'political surplus.' Its justification derives from the latent state of crisis between nations and within every nation . . . The political principle is always stronger in relation to the social principle than the given conditions require. The result is a continuous diminution in social spontaneity.

Ever since I read these words I have found Buber's terminology more valuable as an explanation of events in the real world than many lectures on political theory or sociology. You can see the processes he describes anywhere in the world and they apply with dramatic force to the totalitarian regimes of the 20th century which invariably sought to destroy all those social institutions they could not themselves dominate. I notice among political thinkers, many decades after Buber, the use of the phrase "civil society" to describe what he meant by "society" and applying it in particular when discussing the collapse of the Communist Party institutions in the former Soviet Empire. This links with Kropotkin's view, that I have already mentioned, that we will be compelled to find new forms of organization for the social functions that the state fulfils through the bureaucracy.

*Have you been significantly influenced by any contemporary writers, theorists, or indeed events?*

Yes, I have had innumerable influences, mostly in specific aspects of human life that interest me: for example, architecture and planning, the urban and rural physical environment, children and education, the organization of work, the theory and practice of leaderless groups, and so on. One pair of writers concerned with all these topics were Paul and Percival Goodman and their book *Communitas: Means of Livelihood and Ways of Life* (1947), which for me is one of the most stimulating books of the last century.

I have been influenced by a series of architects, like John Turner, who after his years of work in the *barriadas* of Lima, brought back to Europe the lessons of dweller-built housing in the southern hemisphere, or like another dear friend, the architect Walter Segal. He was born at the anarchist colony of Monte Verità in Ticino, came to Britain as a refugee from Nazism, and late in life devised a very simple but high quality method of house-building which enabled very poor and disadvantaged people to house themselves, *if* they could overcome the bureaucracy.

Among educators I have been much influenced by teachers like A.S. Neill or Dora Russell, who have dared to "set the children free," and like Joe Benjamin, the man who introduced the "adventure playground" to Britain and who used to say, as I've already mentioned, "Children are a modern invention. They used to be part of the family."

Many friends in the world of sociology and criminology have been big influences on me. One is David Downes, a powerful critic of the English penal system; another is Ray Pahl who continually challenges our assumptions about everyday life; and a third is Stanley Cohen, another veteran of the sociology of deviance, who declared in his book *Visions of Social Control* (1985) that "mutual aid, fraternity and good-neighbourliness still sound better than dependence on bureaucracies and professions." His most recent book *States of Denial* (2001) explores one of the most painful of themes: why people and governments deny the existence of atrocities, torture, and legal murder.

I have mentioned to you before that, thanks to Lilian Wolfe of Freedom Bookshop, I read Dwight Macdonald's New York magazine *Politics* from its beginnings in 1944 to its end in 1949, and it influenced me greatly. Other New York intellectuals said of him that he conducted his political education in public, through its pages, from dissident Marxism to implicit anarchism. Paul Goodman was a regular contributor, but Macdonald was unique among American editors in actively seeking European contributors. Some, like George Orwell, George Woodcock, and Alex Comfort were from England, many others were refugees from the horrors of the 1940s, like Hannah Arendt and Bruno Bettelheim. It was in *Politics* too, that I first read Andrea Caffi, Nicola Chiaramonte, Albert Camus, and the political writings of Simone Weil.

A decade later, in 1956, I asked Macdonald why he stopped publishing *Politics* and he simply replied that he had a family to feed. He also said, at the Malatesta Club, that whenever people wanted to discuss with him something that he had written, it was never about what he had said in last week's *New Yorker*, but what he had said years earlier in *Politics* with a circulation that varied between 2,000 and at most 5,000. But it was in *Encounter* in 1957 that he wrote what he later called his most-quoted footnote, observing that

> The revolutionary alternative to the status quo today is not collectivised property administered by a "workers' state" whatever *that* means, but some kind of anarchist decentralisation that will break up mass society into small communities where individuals can live together as variegated human beings instead of as impersonal units in the mass sum. The shallowness of the New Deal and the British Labour Party's postwar regime is shown by their failure to improve any of the important things in people's lives—the actual relationships on the job, the way they spend their leisure, and child-rearing and sex and art. It is mass living that vitiates all these today and the State that holds together the status quo. Marxism glorifies "the masses" and endorses the State. Anarchism leads back to the individual and the community, which is "impractical" but necessary—that is to say, it is revolutionary.

*And Lewis Mumford, the prolific American writer on cities, who became closely associated with the Garden City movement? Did he have an influence on your outlook?*

George Woodcock's wartime articles on regionalism introduced me to Mumford's book *The Culture of Cities*, to the work of the Regional Planning Association of America, and to the ideas of Patrick Geddes, so I owe Mumford a lot.

As long ago as 1948 I wrote to ask Mumford to contribute an introduction to a new Freedom Press edition of *Mutual Aid*, and he replied that "I shall be very proud to have anything of mine appear under the imprint of a press that Kropotkin helped to found." Sadly, that edition did not appear until 1987, and had an introduction by John Hewetson, instead of Mumford.

However, when Freedom Press celebrated its centenary in 1996, Vernon Richards decided to mark the occasion, as well as Mumford's ninetieth birthday, with a reprint of the second half of his book from 1934, *Technics and Civilisation*, and I was asked to write a fourteen-page introduction about the significance of Mumford's work, including his comments in *The Myth of the Machine* (1967) on

> the mass atrocities coldbloodedly perpetrated with the aid of napalm bombs and defoliating poisons, by the military forces of the United States on the helpless peasant populations of Vietnam: an innocent people, uprooted, terrorised, poisoned and roasted alive in a futile attempt to make the power fantasies of the American military-industrial-scientific elite "credible."

His importance for me was that he had a similar message for a much wider readership.

*And how about events?*

One of the problems of being an anarchist journalist is that responses to events are not spontaneous, like the response I quoted to you from my friend John Hewetson to the fall of Ceaucescu. They are all conditioned by thoughts about how to discuss them from an anarchist point of view. Endless events were important simply because they had to happen: for example, the slow withdrawal of British power from the former colonial empire, and the slow collapse of the Soviet Empire too. I could certainly share the delight of those who felt liberated by the protracted deaths of Franco or Stalin and the eventual collapse of the Berlin Wall.

*What about convergences with contemporaries? I've always thought, for example, that you and Michael Young had a lot in common.*

Michael Young (1915–2002) was a sociologist who founded, and until shortly before his death directed, the Institute of Community Studies in East London. He invented the word meritocracy in a famous satire published in 1958, *The Rise of Meritocracy*. The point of Michael Young's book was to project into the future the doctrine of equality of opportunity. Its imaginary author looks back from the revolution of 2033 to the period following the Second World War when "two contradictory principles for legitimising power were struggling for mastery—the principle of kinship and the principle of merit." Merit wins in the end, and with the perfection of methods of intelligence-testing, and consequently with earlier and earlier selection, a new non-self-perpetuating elite is formed, consisting of "the five per cent of the population who know what five per cent means." The top jobs go to the top brains, and Payment by

Merit (according to the formula M = IQ plus Effort) widens the gap between top and bottom people. The people at the bottom are not only treated as inferior: they know they are inferior. But to select the few is to reject the many, and in the meritocratic society of the future new social tensions arise. Although the new working class no longer has men of outstanding intellectual ability, since these have been creamed off by selection, a Populist movement arises, consisting of dissident intellectuals, mainly women, who declare, in their *Chelsea Manifesto* of the year 2009:

> The classless society would be one which both possessed and acted upon plural values. Were we to evaluate people, not according to their intelligence and their education, their occupation and their power, but according to their kindliness and their courage, their imagination and sensibility, their sympathy and generosity, there could be no classes. Who would be able to say that the scientist was superior to the porter with admirable qualities as a father, or the civil servant with unusual skill at gaining prizes superior to the lorry-driver with unusual skill at growing roses? The classless society would also be the tolerant society, in which individual differences were actively encouraged as well as passively tolerated, in which full meaning was at last given to the dignity of man. Every human would then have equal opportunity, not to rise up in the world in the light of any mathematical measure, but to develop his own special capacities for leading a rich life.

This, of course, was regarded as merely sentimental by the meritocrats of the future, until the Populist insurrection of 2034 . . .

Michael Young lived to see the word that he coined, meritocracy, become part of many languages, and to observe (in the *Guardian*, 29 June 2001) that "Too much of what I predicted has become horribly true." He described how the business and professional elite have found a series of new ways of grabbing more and more money, creating an ever-widening gulf between the affluent and the poor, while there is not a word of criticism from the Labour government, "largely filled, as it is, with members of the meritocracy."

*All this reminds me of the "tip," or hint, that you chose for that collection* Seize the Day *(London: Chatto and Windus, 2001).*

I will have to explain that this was a book sponsored by the Institute for Social Inventions, in which 366 "famous and 'extraordinary ordinary' people" were asked to provide a piece of wisdom for each day of the year. I was given Harriet's birthday to celebrate, so my wise saying was a remark she made in the 1970s: "As the threshold of competence rises, so the pool of inadequacy widens."

The comment that I added was precisely that which Michael Young would have made about the widening gulf between the affluent and powerful and the poor and powerless. "Today you have to be far smarter to get by, and if you are not, we penalise your children."

And in case the purchasers of that book might be out of touch with social realities, I drew attention at the bottom of the page to the fact that one-third of all the children in Britain grow up in poverty—with all that this implies about their attainments, behaviour and attitudes—while the gulf between the incomes and opportunities of the affluent and the poor has widened considerably over the past twenty years. The number of households with less than half the average income has risen during that period from four million to eleven million. Meanwhile the confident and competent can rejoice in their instant communication by e-mail or fax. It enables them to ignore those fellow citizens who lack a telephone or bank account and haven't even a toehold in the world they take for granted.

*However, Michael Young has yet another reputation in Britain, hasn't he?*

Yes, this is as an initiator of new, unofficial, organisations which, in Kropotkin's definition of anarchism "would represent an interwoven network, composed of an infinite variety of groups and federations of all sizes and degrees . . . temporary or more of less permanent . . . for all possible purposes . . ."

He founded the Consumers' Association and the Advisory Centre for Education. He played a large part in the origination of the Open University, and was involved in a series of less dramatically successful innovations. One of these was to initiate the Mutual Aid Centre, "set up to try to apply the principles of Robert Owen and Peter Kropotkin in a series of demonstration projects." Its pamphlet from 1980, *Mutual Aid in a Selfish Society,* mentioned how

> It has started a motorists' co-operative offering the
> most up-to-date equipment in Britain for do-it-your-
> self car repairs, a parent-teacher co-operative in a
> Cambridge village school, and a mutual aid centre
> for the exchange of services between tenants in a
> Birmingham tower block, with its own neighbour-
> hood radio station. It has also started a domestic

appliance repair co-operative in Shrewsbury. The projects are all on a small scale, but those which succeed could help to show the way forward for consumer co-operation in Britain.

Michael Young and I tended to meet only about once a decade, so our conversations were usually about what one or the other of us had last written. I remember a meeting when we chanced to be on the same long-distance train from Devon where I had been visiting granddaughters. When we arrived in London another man who had been sitting with us in the train said,

Please forgive me for being so inquisitive, but the books you were talking about sounded so interesting that I would be so grateful if you could tell me the titles and authors.

We did so, feeling ashamed that we had not drawn our fellow-passenger into our conversation. Michael felt even more guilty than me, because the first pamphlet from his Mutual Aid Centre was called *Go to Work on a Brain Train*, describing how regular commuters had set up "Co-operative Learning Clubs" operating on train journeys.

*I consider that you, Noam Chomsky, and Murray Bookchin are the outstanding living libertarian thinkers. Would you provide your assessment of each of the others?*

I have to remind you again that I am not a great thinker. I simply apply a few basic anarchist ideas to the ordinary situations of life. Plenty of the ideas of both Chomsky and Bookchin are incomprehensible to me, even when they are discussing something simple like anarchism. But both of them are unique, at least in the English-speaking world in that, unlike the rest of us, they have broken through the sound barrier that limits other anarchists to a small minority audience. They have succeeded in battling through to a large minority audience.

I have never met Chomsky, but in the 1960s he would kindly allow me to reprint material of his in *Anarchy*, and one evening in the 1970s, I had a long conversation with him by radio. An Australian radio station had an evening devoted to investigating anarchism, interviewing Noam in Boston and me in a studio in London. There were several long intervals when the station was transmitting other material while he and I remained in touch with each other, talking mainly about influences and books. I enjoy the idea of Chomsky as a boy, taking the train to New York to sit around at the office and bookshop of the Yiddish-language anarchist newspaper *Fraye Arbeter Shtime* (Free Voice of Labour), where Rudolf Rocker serialized his book on Anarcho-Syndicalism, and when he took home a different slant on the Spanish war and revolution than that of the Marxist and liberal press. Diego Abad de Santillan's *After the Revolution*, published in New York in 1937, was the basis of Chomsky's observation that "What attracts me about anarchism personally are the tendencies in it that try to come to grips with the problem of dealing with complex organised industrial societies within a framework of free institutions and structures." His own field of propaganda has been different. He has become world-famous as a devastating critic of the foreign and domestic policies of United States governments, their appalling record of intervention in the poor world, and the ways with which the governmental elite in partnership with the military-industrial complex has enlisted both the media and the academic world in the process of "manufacturing consent."

Chomsky says that he is barred from access to the major American journals but this hardly matters since vast numbers of minority journals and publishers are eager to interview him or disseminate his views. He has broken through the barrier of exclusion of dissenting voices.

In 2001 the sociologist Laurie Taylor reported in his BBC radio program "Thinking Aloud" that Noam Chomsky is "the eighth most quoted author of all time" and that "Typing his name into the Internet produces 58,700 references." This is impressive testimony to Chomsky's vigilance and persistence in publicizing the truth about the foreign and domestic policies of successive United States governments.

When Murray Bookchin came clattering into our living room like an urban guerrilla, thirty-five years ago, his appearance belied his message which was that successive waves of fashionable radicalism had failed to address the crisis of American cities. "Far more than the flowers of the mid-sixties," he claimed, "the angry clenched fists of the late sixties were irrelevant in trying to reach an increasingly alarmed and uncomprehending public." I was very grateful in those years for the opportunity to publish in *Anarchy* some important essays of his, for example his account of "Ecology and Revolutionary Thought."

I am quite happy that we only meet every fifteen years or so, because we enquire about health and family rather than about those things which might unite or divide us. Because I have noticed how other anarchists who happen not to share his opinions, at any particular time in their evolution, are trodden into the ground by his denunciations, thus confirming the outside world's view of anarchists as humorless, self-important sectarians.

As a propagandist myself, I value other propagandists by their effectiveness in winning uncommitted people to an anarchist standpoint. This is where Murray has been invaluable. Many of us believe that the kind of issues summed up in shorthand words like *green*, *ecological*, *environmental*, or *sustainable* will be dominant in the politics of the 21st century, and consequently we want to hear convincing anarchist voices in the discussion of these themes. This is precisely what Murray has been providing since the 1960s and he has won an audience, which even though it represents a small minority, has stretched far beyond the range of most of us anarchist propagandists.

George Orwell used to remark about the people he knew who in one decade were calling for global revolution and in the next were, as he put it, "praising God in corduroys." Plenty of Americans have shifted from involvement in social issues to a sentimental and privileged idealization of "wilderness" and the natural environment, with a consequent misanthropy towards their fellow humans. Murray's work has been a splendid challenge to their abandonment of social concerns.

The fact that his early books had examined environmental issues that few people, other than Rachel Carson, were concerned with in the 1950s and 1960s gave Murray a forerunner status in the emerging American green movement, and he linked this with the tradition of home-grown anarchism. "What we are trying to do," he explained (I don't remember where),

> is to redeem certain aspects of the American Dream. There are, of course, several American dreams: one is the John Wayne tradition of the cowboy going out to the West and the whole notion of pioneering individualism; another is the immigrant American dream, this being the land of opportunity where the streets are made of gold. But there is a *third*

American dream, which is the oldest of the lot, dating back to Puritan times, which stresses community, decentralisation, self-sufficiency, mutual aid, and face-to-face democracy.

This is where Murray came into conflict with yet another American dream. For as ecological awareness spread among the children of the affluent, the national guilt over the genocide of indigenous peoples led to an exaltation of the Noble Savage, and a distaste for ordinary mortals who hadn't got the Message. Deep Ecology became fashionable among those affluent enough to "Get Away From It All" and pursue every kind of mystical belief. Murray responded, just in order to rescue the new environmental consciousness from itself, by firmly re-asserting the notion of Social Ecology, aiming at advancing "a serious challenge to society with its vast, hierarchical, sexist, class-ruled, state apparatus and militaristic history."

I met Murray again at the great anarchist event at Venice in 1984 and my last encounter with him was in 1992, when thanks to good organization by Gideon Kossoff and by you, David, he talked about social ecology at a series of meetings in Cambridge, Leeds, Bristol, and London. Unlike most of the anarchist meeting that I remember, they were remarkably well-attended, with overflow audiences, mostly of eager young people who would otherwise seldom be seen at anarchist meetings. Sales of his books were remarkable!

Reflecting on Chomsky and Bookchin, and their ability to win people to an anarchist point of view, leads us to ask what it was that brought *them* into the anarchist movement. In the case of Chomsky it was Rudolf Rocker, the German editor of the London Yiddish journal *Der Arbeterfraynd* (Workers' Friend) before the First World

War, the spokesman for German anarcho-syndicalism until 1933, and then the "elder statesman" of the Yiddish press in North and South America. As I've already re- called, I myself talked in London at meetings celebrating his 70th birthday and his centenary, and I remember very old people with tears in their eyes, telling me, "Everything I am, I owe to Rocker."

In the case of Bookchin, he tells us himself that,

> The fact is that Kropotkin had no influence on my turn from Marxism to anarchism—nor, for that matter, did Bakunin or Proudhon. It was Herbert Read's "The Philosophy of Anarchism" that I found most useful for rooting the views that I slowly de- veloped over the fifties and well into the sixties in a libertarian pedigree; hence the considerable attention he received in my 1964 essay, "Ecology and Revolutionary Thought." Odd as it may seem, it was my reaction against Marx and Engels's cri- tiques of anarchism, my readings into the Athenian polis, George Woodcock's informative history of an- archism, my own avocation as a biologist, and my studies in technology that gave rise to the views in my early essays—not any extensive readings into the works of early anarchists.[3]

The reason why I stress these recollections of influences is that no academic explorer of anarchist history would pay much attention to Rocker or Read as vital influences, but they, respectively, struck a responsive chord with the widely influential Chomsky and Bookchin. I am reminded

---

3    Murray Bookchin: "Deep Ecology, Anarchosyndicalism, and the Future of Anarchist Thought," in *Deep Ecology and Anarchism: A Polemic* (London: Freedom Press, 1993), 47–58.

that, in the 1950s, the psychologist Tony Gibson conducted a survey of readers of *Freedom*, asking them about their initial interest in anarchist ideas. One reader responded that his interest arose from a friend with whom he shared a common love of chrysanthemums.

Part of the likelihood of the seed falling on fertile ground depends, obviously, on the extent to which it has been disseminated. Chomsky, in one area of criticism, and Bookchin, in another, have reached a wider audience than most anarchist propagandists. We should attempt to learn from them. And at the same time, we should be aware that, while English has become a global language, there is a significant untranslated anarchist literature in other languages.

*Colin, you are such a generous person, always unwilling to be critical of fellow anarchists. Yet you imply that there are "things" which "divide" you from Murray. Is it simply a matter of high theory, of style and of changing opinions, all of which you have touched upon, or do you consider more fundamental issues separate your respective, very distinctive conceptions of anarchism?*

It isn't that I am kind or generous. It is simply that I take seriously the business of being an anarchist propagandist. Nothing makes us more ridiculous in the eyes of the world outside than the internal factional disputes that some anarchists enjoy pursuing. I try to avoid them.

*How do you relate anarchism, social ecology and environmentalism?*

I have mentioned already how happy I was to have the opportunity to assemble an updated version of Kropotkin's

*Fields, Factories and Workshops* in 1974. It was especially interesting to note that when the book was last reprinted at the end of the First World War, a note at the beginning explained that, "It pleads for a new economy in the energies used in supplying the needs of human life, since these needs are increasing and the energies are not inexhaustible."

I cannot think of any other social thinker of those days who was expressing the crisis of resources and consumerism in those terms. Kropotkin himself had been criticized, rightly by Malatesta, for his assumption that redistribution would solve the problems of a revolutionary society. In his collection of Malatesta's writings, *Errico Malatesta: His Life and Ideas* (London: Freedom Press, 1965), Vernon Richards notes that Malatesta

> always pointed out that the characteristic of capitalism is under- rather than over-production, and that it was a mistake to believe that the stocks of food and essential goods in the large cities were sufficient to feed the people for more than a few days. When pressed by Malatesta to investigate the true position, Kropotkin who, in all his writings on the subject, had been a partisan of the *prise au tas* (taking from the warehouses) view, discovered that if the imports of food into England stopped for four weeks everybody in the country would die of starvation; and that in spite of all the warehouses in London, the capital city was never provisioned for much more than three days.

In his last years in Russia, Kropotkin was to abandon his earlier optimism, concluding in a postscript written in December 1919 for the 1921 Russian edition of his *Words of a Rebel*, that ". . . given that more than one-third of the population of Russia and Siberia was *always* in poverty and even lacks bread for three or four months a year" and,

> in a word, given that until now a good third of the population of Europe has lived in poverty and has suffered from the lack of clothing and so on, revolution will lead inevitably to *increased consumption*. The demand for all goods will rise while production will fall, and in the end there will be famine—famine in everything, as is the case today in Russia. There is only one way of avoiding such a famine. We must all understand that as soon as a revolutionary movement begins in a country, the outcome will be successful only if the workers in the factories and in the mills, the peasants, and all the citizens themselves at the start of the movement take the whole economy of the nation into their own hands, if they organise themselves and direct their efforts towards a rapid increase in all production. But *they will not be convinced of this necessity unless* all general problems concerning the national economy, today reserved by long tradition to a whole multitude of ministries and committees, *are put in a simple form before each village and each town, before each factory and mill, as being its own business when they are at last allowed to manage themselves.*

The emphases are Kropotkin's and are a reminder that, while we anticipate a post-consumer society, where every household reduces its demands on the productive system, even the richest nations in the world have vast numbers of families living in poverty. The collapse of the Soviet Union in the 1990s resulted in millions of those Russian citizens who could not get a foothold in the new entrepreneurial economy (and who had often spent years as "non-persons," if not as prisoners and as internal exiles) surviving in the new market economy of entrepreneurial wizards who were frequently their former oppressors among the *apparatchiks* of the old regime, only because of their harvest of potatoes in the vegetable garden.

I think that my own anarchist propaganda was always conscious of Green issues. I was, for example, writing about the significance of solar power, wind power and tidal power in *Freedom* as long ago as 1957 and 1958, when the non-specialist writer had to seek out the esoteric information from the handful of eccentric inventors who were concerned with renewable sources of energy. And then, all through the 1970s, I had the great good fortune to be paid to produce the monthly *Bulletin of Environmental Education* (BEE). I have already mentioned how useful at the time was the *Blueprint for Survival* (1972), reprinted as a mass-circulation paperback. The passage of so many years has not revealed any defects in the *Blueprint*, but it has reminded us that the economics of global capitalism will not admit that there are limits to economic growth.

People who have moved in Green circles for decades can certainly appreciate Murray Bookchin's distinction between Deep Ecology and Social Ecology. We used to be told that mediaeval theologians would discuss topics like the precise number of angels who could dance on the head of a pin, and I have certainly met tedious lovers of paradox who delight in arguments about which form of electronic communication uses fewer natural resources, as though this was a determining factor in human conduct. I see this kind of discussion as frivolous when compared with the real environmental dilemmas that face us.

COLIN WARD & DAVID GOODWAY

In the earliest days of *BEE*, one of our most stimulating mentors was a witty and inventive young man called
Peter Harper, who in 1975 went to Wales to join a group of
enthusiasts who were starting the Centre for Alternative
Technology (CAT) at Llwyngwern Quarry at Machynlleth,
in a landscape of industrial dereliction. Today that enter-
prise (operating as a workers' co-operative of twenty-eight
members) is visited by about 80,000 people every year,
including 20,000 schoolchildren, and is world-famous as
a demonstration site for environmentally friendly power
generation, building construction and sewage disposal. I
am told that "it generates 90 percent of its own energy in
renewable form from sun, wind and water."

Peter Harper has worked at the Centre for Alternative
Technology for over a quarter of a century, and has an-
swered endless questions from students, children, and
curious visitors. At one level I am much impressed by an
answer he gave to interviewers in 1998:

> The craze for self-sufficiency and small-is-beautiful
> has passed. Don't try to do it all yourself. Start where
> you are strong, not where you are weak. In a modern
> society you sell your marketable skills and purchase
> the rest: there are loads of other specialists. Don't
> try to make your energy: try to save your energy.
> Most of the action is going to be in cities, where the
> majority of humans will soon be living and where,
> contrary to our old Arcadian assumptions, sustain-
> able modern lifestyles are more easily achieved.[4]

Long experience of probing the environmental consciousness of our fellow-citizens has led him to make a different

---

4    Interview in W. and D. Schwarz, *Living Lightly: Travels in
Post-Consumer Society*, (Oxford: Jon Carpenter, 1998).

distinction than that between Deep Ecologists and Social Ecologists. Peter divides us between Light Greens (with more money than time) and Deep Greens (with, perhaps, more time than money). The Light Greens, he suggests, are involved with a new technology of solar heating, fuel-efficient, lightweight motor-cars, and sustainable consumption, while the Deep Greens believe in small, insulated houses, bicycles and public transport, home-grown food, repair and recycling, local currency and barter.

Meanwhile, he suggests, the rest of society will continue to belong to the culture of *MORE*! For he observes that

> People aspire to greater convenience and comfort, more personal space, easy mobility, a sense of expanding possibilities. This is the modern consumerist project: what modern societies are all about. It is a central feature of mainstream politics and economics that consumerist aspirations are not seriously challenged. On the contrary, the implied official message is "Hang on in there: we will deliver." The central slogan is brutally simple: *MORE*!

Some of us, Peter Harper noted in his Schumacher Lecture at Bristol in 2001, have apocalyptic visions of uncontrollable catastrophes resulting from indiscriminate economic activity. He, as an optimist, after decades of attempting to demonstrate the potential of alternative technology, thinks that as life gets worse for everyone else, the Deep Greens (the people he calls the recessive genes of the sustainability movement) will be found to have solved what he calls the great riddle of reconciling modernity and sustainability: "They will be quite visibly having a good time: comfortable, with varied lives and less stress, healthy and fit, having rediscovered the elementary virtues of re-straint and balance."

His Deep Greens have a different flavor to that of Murray's Deep Ecologists, but perhaps they too lack the so-cial dimension that is vital for Green propaganda, since the capitalist market economy and the acquisitiveness that feeds it are, precisely, the enemies of the elementary virtues of re-straint and balance that Peter and I both hope to re-assert.

*Do you think that the achievement of an anarchist society is a practical possibility and, if so, how do you conceive it being realized? Or is it, rather, a matter of attaining a more libertarian, less hierarchical society. Would you agree that Western society, at least, has become much freer during the course of your own lifetime?*

Economists talk of "perfect co-operation" as the ideal type for an anarchist society. I do not believe that an anarchist society is a practical possibility, and my lack of belief is not to do with the viability of anarchism but with the na-ture of human societies, since every society that we can imagine in the modern world is a mixture of different, of-ten contradictory tendencies.

For example, before the collapse of the Soviet Union, I used to say that the thing that made life tolerable there was the unacknowledged private market elements that enabled citizens to buy fresh vegetables or razor blades, and that, similarly, the only thing that makes life possible for millions in the United States are its non-capitalist elements. Contrary to rumor, friends tell me that if you collapse in the street there, the hospital treats you before it enquires about your insurance status. Huge areas of life in the United States, and everywhere else, are built around voluntary and mutual aid organizations.

But, yes, of course, life in Western society has become immensely more free in the course of my own adult life. I have already quoted to you Dwight Macdonald's famous footnote about the important things in people's lives: "the actual relationships on the job, the way they spend their leisure, and child-rearing and sex and art"—which have changed immensely since I was young. I would find it difficult to place, in order of significance, the different areas of human freedom which have expanded, in Western society, during the last forty years. But let me try.

The first of these is undoubtedly women's liberation, and with this a series of sexual issues are involved, like the availability of contraception and abortion. But the implications of the women's movement seem to me to be wider. The kinds of anti-social behaviour that makes our fellow-citizens unable to accept the concept of an anarchist society are predominantly male activities. A second expansion of human freedom has been the decriminalization of homosexuality, where in my lifetime vast injustices and cruelties were perpetrated in the name of morality and the law.

The third huge revolution in attitudes relates to the sexual information given to the young. Anarchists, for example Alex Comfort and John Hewetson, were important in ridiculing the myths about masturbation and providing advice about pregnancy and ways of avoiding it. A comparison of statistics about unwanted teenage pregnancies between Britain and, say, the Netherlands and Denmark or Sweden, seems to indicate that the revolution in sexual education has some way to go, but anyone old enough to remember the silent horrors of adolescent pregnancies in the past will know that we have moved a great distance.

The same things applies, almost incidentally, to the abandonment of physical punishment in schools. Even the

English have become more civilized, and the anarchists have been among the civilizing factors.

*But wouldn't you also agree that in many aspects of life there is much less reason for optimism?*

I agree. I have mentioned Dwight Macdonald's remark about actual relationships at the work-place. Their improvement was the result of a century of agitation and organization by the workers' unions, in reducing the length of the working day and week and in improving working conditions. But in the last twenty years of the last century, many of the gains that unions had won have been reversed. British, German, French, or Italian employers can buy the far cheaper labor of workers in China, Malaysia, Vietnam, or Indonesia at a fraction of the cost of labor in the West, and without the conditions of work fought for by generations of union members. Statistics show that people in Britain, and in the U.S., are spending more time at work. Parental time has been stolen from the family because of the demands of employers, and so of course has the time devoted to activities in the community, as the American sociologist Robert Putnam argues.

I told you how lucky I was, in the postwar years of full employment, to be able to drift into a variety of interesting jobs with very little in the form of qualifications, and I told you how I have been much impressed by the idea that happiness in work is related to the "span of autonomy" of the individual worker. All my life, most people had work which may have involved boredom, exhaustion, and long hours. They developed an armory of self-defence and compensations. I get the impression that today's low-grade jobs are without these modifying factors.

*And the issue is made more complex by international migration, where anarchist approaches are inevitably far from popular opinion?*

You are right. A century ago, when much of the globe had been colonized by the British, vast numbers of British people decided that they could improve their prospects in life, emigrating to Canada, South Africa, Australia, and New Zealand. They greatly improved their prospects in life by doing so.

The postal remittances sent home to Britain and Ireland, played a very important part in the economy of the poor. Today the flow of migrants is reversed. Hopeful would-be migrants into Fortress Europe pay huge sums to international crooks, and their sufferings are terrible. These incidents are only publicized when they make news: for example the case in June 2000, when fifty-eight Chinese immigrants to Britain died in a container entering Britain through the Channel Tunnel.

Anarchists, who cannot believe in the validity of state frontiers, are obliged to support the freedom to move from country to country, and can often find support from the economic results of international migration. The ease with which our fellow-citizens become xenophobes is even more disturbing when we consider the circumstances of legally long-established British families who are Black or Asian.

There is an undercurrent in British daily life of attacks on families of a different color, ranging from arson to the murder of teenage boys in the street, by (it is assumed) white boys of a similar age. I tried to come to terms with this issue thirty years ago in the book I edited on vandalism, where I suggested that, all over the world, in situations of communal or "religious" violence or "race riots," the young are not merely the *scapegoats*, but are also the *shock troops* of their elders:

> The resigned and the old are sitting at home hating, while the young, who have not yet learned resignation or prudence, or "responsibility," or acquired responsibilities, are out there fighting.

Business and capital migrate freely around the world, from one continent to another, and a century ago Europeans emigrated everywhere in search of a better life but, if workers and their families seek to move today from the poor world to the rich, they are first exploited by ruthless people-smugglers, and then treated as criminals, and finally abused and exploited again by ruthless employers, under the threat of deportation. Finally, their children are subject to persecution and worse, by their indigenous counterparts.

It would be absurd for anarchists to support any governmental policies designed to prevent the freedom of movement of fellow humans. The fact that our fellow citizens regard such a view as madness is one illustration of how far we still are from impregnating society with anarchist attitudes. But the anarchist voices of the coming century are likely to include those of men and women who came to this country as children in a climate of danger, hostility and permanent insecurity, and will have had to battle their way into our own libertarian tradition.

*I agree, of course, about the invalidity of state frontiers; but, on the other hand, I consider the advocacy of freedom of movement is going to be entirely unrealistic in the 21st century—indeed, even mad! Whereas in the 19th and 20th centuries Europeans were emigrating to underpopulated regions—an existing underpopulation supplemented by ruthless genocide—we are currently entering an era of possibly even larger movements of people; but now from Eastern Europe, Asia, and Africa, to the small and crowded countries of Western Europe. This, I think, together with religious intolerance, constitutes the greatest potential sources of conflict in the coming decades. In any case, I'm bemused by the popularity of Britain as a destination. If I were a migrant I would head for Spain or Italy with a superior quality of life and much better climate, even if with lower benefits!*

It is not a matter of advocacy of freedom of movement. It is a question of not merely popular hostility, but of punitive governmental attitudes. For among the governments of Western Europe there is a form of rivalry, in the effort to prove to their own populations that they are tougher or more ruthless in excluding migrants. The last people to demand that migrants should settle Somewhere Else are surely the anarchists.

The exploitation, dangers, and sufferings of migrant families and the existence of sinister "people-smugglers" are the result of immigration controls imposed by governments.

*I imagine that, like me, you are extremely heartened by the rise of the anti-globalization and anti-capitalist movement. But how do you react to its apparently inescapable violent periphery? Isn't 21st-century anarchism in danger of becoming permanently associated with violence and destruction in just the same way as 20th-century anarchism could not shake off the reputation of terrorism it had acquired in the 1890s? As then, will not the public image of anarchism now alienate it from the bulk of its natural supporters: that is, ordinary, peaceable human beings, anarchism's natural constituency?*

I agree completely that it is good news that every meeting of the World Bank, the International Monetary Fund, the World Trade Organization, and the political bosses of the major industrial countries is met by large-scale anti-capitalist and anti-globalization demonstrations. I also observe an inescapable violent periphery. The British prime minister Tony Blair attributed this to "an anarchist travelling circus that goes from summit to summit," but most observers would see it as an escalation of police determination to keep demonstrators away from their political and economic rulers. It was reported, for example, in the *Guardian* for 3 July 2001 that "the police methods of restraint are becoming increasingly violent. They have used dogs, horses and tear gas. At the Gothenburg demonstration, three protesters were shot and wounded by the police." Then on 20 July 2001, at Genoa, the Carabinieri shot and killed a twenty-year-old demonstrator.

In preparation for the protests at Genoa, the Milan anarchist monthly "*A*" (*revista anarchica*), no. 274, Summer 2001, included an 8,000-word bilingual supplement, edited by Adriano Paolella and Zelinda Carloni, called *Globalisation: Ideas for Understanding, Living with and Opposing the New Model of Profit-Making*. They completely agree with you and me about the capitalist travelling circus that goes from summit to summit, and they had important things to say about violence, with which you and I would agree. They note that we are all rightly outraged by the way that a small handful of people influence every minute of ordinary life, controlling our future with absolute arrogance. So they understand that we would all like chance to demonstrate our opposition, but they add that those who cannot control their temper might as well stay at home, because violent action reduces the significance of the opposition. And they added that

> It is harmful because it is so often desired, support-
> ed, defended and promoted by governments who
> have already (and particularly in Italy) recognised
> the advantages of shifting attention from the true
> issue to violent conflict.

But even this case brings us a dilemma. In October and November 2001 a series of demonstrations marched through central London in opposition to the bombing of Afghanistan by Britain and America. The first of these major demonstrations, attended by a vast range of opponents, was totally unreported, even in the left-wing press, for example the *Guardian*. Readers protested, and the second demonstration, similarly entirely free of conflict with the police, was fulsomely reported in that newspaper. If a single government or McDonald's window had been broken, those demonstrations would have become *news*.

You and I have seen the same suppression of news about non-sectarian protests in Northern Ireland, or about the Peace Movement's protests in Israel. We do not have an answer to this problem, although users of the Internet believe that they do have.

*But what about the renewed association of anarchism with unacceptable violence in the minds of ordinary people?*

Ordinary people may also have no idea why anyone should object to the activities of the International Monetary Fund or the World Bank. However, all my own propaganda over many years has been directed at changing the minds of ordinary people.

*You once told me that all your publications were "looking at life from an anarchist point of view"; and indeed I recall you introducing yourself (at the History Workshop at Salford University) as "an anarchist propagandist." More recently you seem to have changed your position by saying that all your books "hang together as an exploration of the relations between people and their environment." Is there a contradiction here or do you stand by all three statements?*

Yes indeed: I have forgotten the occasions, but these statements are all true. The first remark is inevitably correct because we could all be placed on a sliding scale between authoritarians and libertarians in our attitudes to life and the problems that it raises, and my books belong to the libertarian end of this scale. The second is bound to be true because all these books, like those of any writer, are to persuade the reader to agree with me. And the third is an accurate description of the kind of books I write.

My books exist because some publisher or research body commissioned them, but they are unmistakably the work of an anarchist. As an example, there is a book club, producing handsome editions of, mostly, standard classics, called the Folio Society. I have edited and introduced a number of books for them, from Kropotkin's *Memoirs* to *Huckleberry Finn*. Once a year they publish for their members a beautifully illustrated original book. In 1985 they offered me £2,500 to write such a book about the building of Chartres Cathedral in France. (In addition, of course, Harriet and I had two immensely enjoyable visits there.) The book that resulted fitted all three of my contradictory statements. The approach to the medieval city, followed of course, Kropotkin's characterisation of "an art which sprang out of the *social* life of the city." It evoked the celebration, by thinkers like William Morris, of the craft organization of the city's builders, and it ended with a celebration of a modern "naïve" artist, the man employed to sweep the paths of the cemetery at Chartres. His name was Raymond Isidore (1900–1964) and the last page of my book explains that

> In 1928 he built his own house in the Rue de Repos, and proceeded to cover the walls, inside and out, as well as the garden walls, with a mosaic of bits of broken glass, china, ceramics, anything durable, to form a series of elaborate designs and pictures, mostly of the cathedral and of daily life and work. In a way it glows with the same overpowering plenitude as the cathedral itself. The neighbours called him Picassietta, which means scrounger.

Most of my books, including my collaborations with Dennis Hardy and David Crouch, tend to be explorations of the "unofficial" environment, recognized as re-assertions of popular sovereignty.

*I am delighted that you finally found a publisher for* Cotters and Squatters. *Why do you experience such problems with publishers? And please tell me what* Cotters and Squatters *is about.*

This book celebrates the legacy of the folklore, found in Europe (as well as in the former Turkish empire) that, if a house can be erected between sundown and sunrise with a saucepan boiling by the morning, then the occupants cannot be evicted. I gathered material about squatter houses in England and Wales for this book for many years, although I could not afford to spend much on visits to sites and to archives. But it does resurrect a lost chapter in popular history and is yet another exploration of popular and unofficial involvement in the environment, like so many of my books, from *Vandalism* and *The Child in the City* onwards.

It was rejected by about ten major publishers, but appeared from a friend who, after working in an alternative bookshop in Nottingham for many years, established Five Leaves Publications in that city. I am sure that one important reason why my books are seen as a problem by publishers is simply that they take a long time to sell! Another is that it is hard to predict on which shelf, either in bookshops or libraries, they belong. My books tend to earn a great deal of praise but small sales and little money. But books, simply because they have a longer life than journalism and find a place on library and bookshop shelves, have a wonderful way of continuing to reach people over the years. Let me give you an example.

In the 1960s Penguin Books started their Education Division, and in the 1970s, under new ownership, closed it down. But in those ten years Penguin Education produced some brilliantly innovative series of school books. Among them was the *Connexions* series, edited by Richard Mabey, intended to entice reluctant readers aged fourteen and upwards. He entrusted me with two of the most awkward topics, the book on violence and the one on work. They were widely used, among students both older and younger than the intended audience, and were reprinted by Penguin every year all through the 1970s. I used to claim that my *Work* was the only honest school book about work that at that time had been written.

Over the last thirty years I have continually met people who had encountered my name and my photograph from the covers of those little books. I remember in the 1980s I had a letter from a reader. He had read *Work*, not as a schoolchild but as an employed adult. It had changed his life, he said, and he had never worked since. Should I have felt gratified, or horrified, or guilty? He meant, of course, that he had ceased to be employed, and was working for himself and his family. His letter was, all the same, a sharp reminder of the responsibilities that propagandists accumulate.

In 1998 I was talking at a meeting in Trieste organised by the group who publish the anarchist journal *Germinal* in that city. The occasion was the appearance from Elèuthera of their second edition of the Italian version of my book *Freedom to Go: After the Motor Age* that Freedom Press published in 1991. Despite its regrettably Anglocentric character, it was translated into Italian in 1992, into French in 1993, and into Spanish in 1996. In a celebration for the reprinted Italian text I had been talking about the emergence in Britain of direct action anti-road protesters. "Other fields of popular protest may be dormant," I said, "but proposals for new roads have led to groups of objectors digging tunnels or building houses in trees in order to impede the road-building contractors." And I explained that young, witty, and resourceful protesters, even though eventually driven out, had begun the process of changing the nation's opinion on new roads. With nicknames like "Animal" or "Swampy," they were not ridiculed, but had become the temporary heroes of the popular press and television. Was this a significant trend?

When people at the meeting were asked to comment, one man spoke with passion and I could not understand what he was saying. My kind translator, Giorgio

Cingolani, explained that this new friend was not talking about transport, but about the fact that, years earlier he had bought my little book on violence, and the photograph on the cover of me with a baby, carried in a sling on my back, had permanently affected his attitude to child-rearing.

Books have unexpected consequences!

*What about the books you always meant to write but never have done?*

People like us need to remind ourselves that anarchists have a certain "scarcity value" in our society, and some of us, like me, forget this and spend too much time on marginal topics, simply because that is where we can find an audience. I'm aware of having devoted more energy than was sensible on trying to change official attitudes to housing. The only reward is that assertion of the principle of dweller control is frequently referred to as an anarchist notion, associated with John Turner and me.

A book that I would have liked some publisher to commission from me is a discussion of boys. Because of the publication of my book *The Child in the City*, in both the 1979 and 1990 editions, I was continually asked to address meetings and discussions with educators and sociologists, and had to conceal my ignorance of the vast research findings on gender differences. So I was bold enough to make the subject of my lecture at the Anarchist Book Fair in London in 1997, "Bad Boys: Anarchism and Gender Assumptions." But by now, I have really left such an exploration too late.

If I were better organized I would have written an anarchist book about federalism. You probably have the same experience as me. We are strong critics of the

Euro-bureaucracy and aware that all our politicians are illiterate about the principles of federalism, and consequently find ourselves with reactionary neighbors asserting nonsense about *Great* Britain. Plenty of anarchist thought on the federal principle exists, from for example Camillo Berneri in the past down to the Dutch anarchist Thom Holterman in the present, whose analysis I tried to publicise in *Freedom* and *The Raven*. I would like, at last, to produce in English, a simple and accessible anarchist discussion of the federal principle.

*I am surprised you do not mention the name of Proudhon.*

Well, you will not be surprised that I find him a difficult writer, even in English translation. However, about fifteen years ago I discovered an English translation of his *The Principle of Federation*, published in 1979 by the University of Toronto Press, and resolved to discuss the topic in a modern way.

*So we can expect a work on federalism? Are there any other books we can look forward to from you?*

I dare not say "No," because in the unlikely event of a commercial publisher commissioning a book, I would probably accept. Vernon Richards was continually urging me to put together books of my lectures for Freedom Press because he imagined that this would entail a minimum of work.

*Why are you always quoting other people?*

I usually find that another writer has expressed some idea or other far better than I could do myself, so I am happy to quote them, *always* with acknowledgement. Perhaps I was asleep in the classroom on the day we were taught the art of summarizing or of précis, which is an art I have always found difficult. But I have never learned that it is undesirable to quote other writers. I do not put a high value on originality and as a propagandist I *do* find it important to discover and pass on a convincing argument. As Montaigne said, "I quote others only the better to express myself."

*That is a splendid defense of a "bad habit"! Have you ever thought of writing fiction?*

You will have noticed that I am a very prosaic writer, but I do sometimes have an idea that would make a good novel. I have actually known several novelists, from Colin MacInnes to Ruth Rendell, and if I should ever say to one of them, "Here's a great plot for you. There was this man who . . . ," then they look at me pityingly and say: "Colin, you are full of good ideas, but you haven't *any* idea of how a novelist sets to work."

However, I will tell you about the novel that has been at the back of my mind for many years. It is about a man who has been released from the only psychiatric prison in Britain, and has been told by the psychiatrist that it would be therapeutic for him to adopt a hobby of collecting. There are collectors of everything: books, postage stamps, coins, beer-mats, and so on. He decides to become the world's first collector of seed-packets, because as a child he had always enjoyed the pictures and photolithography on seed packets, so he set out on travels among gardeners in order to gather these ephemeral items, and the book would be a picaresque account of his wanderings among gardeners and their greenhouses.

The moment I tell you about the setting of my never-written novel, you can see how unsuited I would be to attempt to become a writer of fiction.

My unwritten novel has an interesting background but no plot!

*But all the same, it starts in a specific place: the psychiatric prison called Grendon Underwood. Why?*

Anarchists have always been interested in prison systems, partly because they have frequently been victims, and partly because they have dared to propagate the idea of human societies without penal sanctions and consequently have to suggest alternative approaches to their sceptical readers. The first experiences have led to several anarchist classics like Kropotkin's *In Russian and French Prisons* (1887) and Alexander Berkman's *Prison Memoirs of an Anarchist* (1912).

My own penal experience was limited to a brief incarceration at a Military Detention Camp in the Orkney Islands (56 days) for a ludicrous military offence. My fellow prisoners, I quickly found, conformed to the stereotype of victims, being either too slow or too maladroit to keep out of trouble. Some seemed to be quite mad, and plenty of them were younger than me. Some were Irish (the Irish Republic was a neutral country in the Second World War) and had joined the British army as boys, to get away from orphanages run by the Christian Brothers in Ireland. I would have expected their background to have taught them the art of avoiding trouble. But they seemed to be automatic victims of the military machine.

In Britain, the important mentors of penal reform were those objectors to military service in the First World War who were given long and sometimes repeated prison sentences in ordinary jails. Several of them became life-long advocates of attempts to transform prisons from punitive to therapeutic institutions. There are also plenty of critics, including me, who declare that this transformation is impossible, but who at the same time have eagerly watched these experiments, just because they are more civilized than the barbaric, punitive role of prisons.

But anarchists have always been interested in the variety of experiments that heroic pioneers have undertaken with young delinquents in developing autonomy and self-organisation. Some were described in my book *Anarchy in Action* where I mentioned the paradox that the British and Australian armies adopted the technique of the "leaderless group," as a means of selecting leaders, and were followed in this by the theorists of industrial management. I am sure that the psychiatrists in the prison that was the starting-point of the character in my unwritten novel were seeking ways of encouraging autonomous personalities. There are echoes of this in the book presented to me, in which you were a contributor.

*This was* Richer Futures: Fashioning a New Politics, *edited by Ken Worpole (London: Earthscan, 1999), intended as "a common wish by a number of people active in various educational, social and environmental initiatives to pay tribute to the writer Colin Ward." What did you feel about it?*

Obviously I was immensely gratified by this *festschrift*, most of all because among the contributors were some people whose activities I had admired for years, but had never met or corresponded with, who said that they felt that I was a friend. For me this was a marvellous revelation. One of those contributors, Professor Tim Lang, who is an authority on the politics and ethics of food, wrote that

> Even in these televisual times, the relationship between reader and author can be intensely personal. In a world which is said to be more individualised, atomised and socially fragmented, the relationship between reader and writer takes on new poignancy. It is one of the great anonymous relationships of the modern world.

The response to that book from reviewers was also interesting for me. For example, in a journal called *Therapeutic Communities* it was reviewed by the head of psychotherapy at The Retreat in York.

That reviewer found that he had the sensation of "meeting people digging a tunnel towards the therapeutic community from another place in society with the same basic idea." And he went on to explain that my anarchism

> is all about ways of enabling people to take control of their lives and participate in the decision-making processes that affect them—in education, housing, the environment built and natural, food, even how water supplies are managed.

I, of course, was gratified that the connections that I was attempting to build in the journal *Anarchy* in the 1960s, and later in the book *Anarchy in Action*, between anarchist ideology and the experience of those people who were brave enough to set up self-governing, non-punitive communities of "delinquent" youngsters, were at last recognized outside the anarchist movement. I also learned that there is an archive housing the records of these experiments. This is the Planned Environment Therapy Trust, Church Lane, Toddington, Cheltenham GL54 5DQ.

*Of the millions of words you have written (or quoted) in the past half-century, most have been produced in the form of regular "columns" of one kind or another. Would you tell me something about your life as a columnist?*

I think I spent the late 1940s in searching around for the right format for my contributions to *Freedom* and it must have been after the change from fortnightly to weekly publication in 1951 that I settled into the habit of a weekly column of a long, reflective kind, which in the middle 1950s acquired the heading "People and Ideas." I would notice, because of the overseas papers that arrived at the Freedom Bookshop, that my column was often translated in journals like *L'Adunata* or the *Fraye Arbeter Shtime* in New York and *La Protesta* or *Dos Fraye Vort* in Buenos Aires.

I did not know then, but learned later, that market research in the ordinary press shows that most readers of any journal turn first to the columnists. Neither *Anarchy* in the 1960s, nor *BEE* in the 1970s, had a regular column.

But by this time I was being asked to contribute columns to non-anarchist journals. The most significant of these was the sociological weekly *New Society* with which I had a good relationship from its inception in the early 1960s onwards. For years I contributed odd news items on issues like education, delinquency, housing, and planning, and I was very happy to be asked in the 1970s to be asked to join the rota of contributors to the full-page "Stand" column in that journal. This led to long debates with a very intelligent and well-informed readership, and led to interesting correspondence and invitations to address other audiences elsewhere. My good luck continued when in 1988 *New Society* was amalgamated with the *New Statesman*, a very old-established socialist journal, to form *New Statesman and Society*. I was given the opportunity to write a weekly column under the title "Fringe Benefits."

This gave me a wider audience than I had ever had, as well as doubling my weekly income. I lasted for 400 weeks under three editors, but in 1996, the journal changed ownership, and, together with most of the other regular contributors, I was instantly dismissed by the new editor.

Meanwhile, of course, I had been a columnist in several other journals. At several times in its history I have been a contributor to various columns in the long-established weekly *Architects' Journal*, and from 1979 to the present day I have written a monthly column, also called "People and Ideas," in *Town and Country Planning*. From 1993 to 1999 I wrote a regular "Anarchist Notebook" in the fortnightly *Freedom*. Quite often the same story was the subject of my column in several different journals, because, I argued, the overlap of circulation was either minimal or non-existent.

I was, in my view, propagating an anarchist approach in columns or articles in a variety of journals concerned with architecture, planning and housing, and I always sought this kind of niche in education journals too. For about twenty years I reviewed thousands of books in the leading journal for teachers, the *Times Educational Supplement*, but never achieved a regular slot. My aim was, as always, to make the anarchist approach a point of view that was taken seriously in every field of social life. I want anarchist attitudes to be among those that citizens everywhere know about, and cannot dismiss as an amusing curiosity of the political fringe.

*In the ten years when you produced* Anarchy, *you never published a story, you hardly ever published anything that could be called "literary criticism" and only in one issue did you publish any poetry. Have you a bias against literature?*

No. But you will know that anyone who edits any specialist journal, whether it is about gardening or football, is besieged by poets, enclosing at least ten flower-smelling or goal-keeping poems. An anarchist editor would have the intolerable task of assessing the "anarchy-quotient" of material submitted, and most of us know, from having been subjected to it, that propagandist poetry is usually rather poor poetry.

On the one occasion when an issue of *Anarchy* was devoted to poetry, they were the poems smuggled out of prison, written by a young man whose crime was setting fire to the Imperial War Museum in London. I should add that this museum houses the testimony of opposition to the two world wars, as well as military material.

*But they keep it well hidden!*

True. But to my knowledge, their oral archive has collected the recorded testimony of John Hewetson, Philip Sansom, and probably other anarchists as well as me.

However, it was sound sense for me to avoid "creative writing" in *Anarchy*. With a title like that, authors would be sending me avant-garde literature intended to shock the bourgeoisie, without regard for the fact that artists of all sorts have been shocking the bourgeoisie for a century, and that the rest of us find it hard to suppress a yawn.

I could have been less doctrinaire about poetry, but I would then have been faced with the odious task of deciding what to reject and what to print. You and I would probably agree that the most distinguished English poet of the postwar decades was Philip Larkin, whose political opinions, however, were not merely odious, but nauseous. But there was quite often a half-page to fill at the end of an article which could have contained a poem. My punishment for my policy was that I have always kept in my head a little four-line verse sent to me by the poet Oonagh Lahr, and automatically rejected by me. She wrote:

> One who on hard beds
> Slept long and deep
> Now on a softer bed
> Cannot sleep.

I should have published it!

*I know Oonagh rather well; and I guess this stems from one of her spells of imprisonment arising from the "sit-downs" of the Committee of 100 against nuclear weapons. But what are your literary tastes: in fiction and poetry? Do you have time nowadays to read creative writing—or is it a matter of keeping up with professional "literature"? Have drama and the theatre even been of importance to you? And what about the cinema? I know you have been an avid filmgoer in your time.*

You have to remember that propagandists are not useful critics. All through the 1950s and 1960s, in reading a novel, hearing a poem, or seeing a play or a film, I would be unconsciously measuring its AQ (anarchy-quotient) and the extent to which this could be exploited in my propaganda. By the 1970s, I had added to this the factor of EQ (environmental-quotient) and exploiting this too.

Being blessed with musical children, many of our evenings in the 1970s were spent in taking them to performances or hearing them and their friends perform. In the past twenty years, living deep in the country, we have very seldom been to the theatre, though seeing the same television as everyone else. For Harriet and for me, it is a major pleasure to take the bus to the Ipswich Film Theatre (run by the local council in our nearest town) to see all those films from around the world that the commercial cinema ignores.

We have been thrilled, for example, by the current Iranian cinema, where the film-makers seem to have been probing the limits of the choices of topic they are able to explore.

The kind of novels that I borrow from the public library are probably the same as the ones you read: let us say the books of Rose Tremain or Ian McEwan or the Irish novelist Bernard MacLaverty.

*You have always been busy as a speaker, as I know from the series of books from Freedom Press consisting of lectures given in several countries on a variety of occasions: for example,* Talking Houses, Talking to Architects, *and* Talking Schools.

Yes, I am not a good speaker, although I know a few essentials like the need to talk loudly, to repeat vital facts, and to ensure that every member of the audience has a piece of paper with further references. So I always have a prepared text, even though I may depart from it on the occasion. And like anyone who talks a lot in public, I repeat variants on the same lecture. As a result I have accumulated a series of texts which, when Freedom Press asks for a book, can always be gathered together.

I think that Kropotkin wrote somewhere that economy was the art of maximum use. I try very hard to get the maximum use of everything I have written or said, exposing it before different audiences and occasions.

We anarchist propagandists have to "trundle our little wheelbarrow of propaganda" as somebody said (was it Herbert Read or George Orwell?), so we have to empty it where it will be most effective.

But you must have had the same experience as me, or as any anarchist speaker, that years later somebody says to you, "What you said was so important in my life, because I had never before come across your point of view." My response is usually the same as yours, or that of anyone else: "If only I had known, I would have said it better!"

However, the spoken voice, addressing endless small audiences, is as important today as it ever was in the history of anarchist propaganda. What I have never been very good at, even when I was a teacher, is the technique for drawing maximum participation out of the group. I have an American friend, Taylor Stoehr (the editor of the works of Paul Goodman), who described his teaching technique to me in a recent letter:

> My strategy is to begin each meeting with a single written question that seems to me to go to the heart of the matter. I ask students to spend ten minutes writing their answers, then divide them into groups of four to discuss the various issues that arise when they compare their answers. After half an hour the classroom is buzzing, as they wrestle with the real concerns that they've unearthed. *Everyone* participates—there are no quiet ones in the back of the room with this approach. And because I remove my own authority (I just sit on the desk and

> eavesdrop), they can work towards the level and
> kind of understanding appropriate to their actual
> readiness for the ideas—something they can help
> each other with much more than I can.

Taylor Stoehr went on to describe to me his belief that genuine and permanent learning can take place in this situation, whereas, he argues, "so very little results from a lecture or even a good group discussion, which invariably leaves most people out." I wish that I had been given this advice, and taken notice of it, in the days when I first became a teacher and lecturer. One thing I enjoy doing, when my hosts allow it, is to tell an audience that I propose to reverse the usual procedure, and to begin with the questions and follow that with the lecture. Invariably one question leads to another and the dialogue completely replaces the lecture, with (so long as the room or hall is acoustically adequate) greater satisfaction for the participants. Of course, the bigger the room, the less possibility there is of any real dialogue. Paul Goodman wrote a great essay on this theme, called "Seating Arrangements: An Elementary Lecture in Functional Planning," which I once helped the poet Adrian Mitchell to present on television by moving the studio audience around.

*You mentioned that you have been asked to lecture for at least a quarter of a century on the theme of* The Child in the City. *But during that time the experiences of children as well as your own observations must have changed?*

Yes, I have had to discuss that book with every kind of audience, from policemen to fourteen-year-olds. These kids of course were convulsed with laughter at the clothes and hair-styles of the children of twenty years earlier in

the marvellous photographs by Ann Golzen in the original edition. I had been convinced that the photographs
would have been more effective than the text in convey-
ing the intensity, variety, and ingenuity of the experience
of urban childhood, and I mentioned in introducing the
second English edition that, when I discussed the book
with meetings of teachers and social workers, I found
that they perceived it as one more catalog of urban de-
privations, rather than as the celebration of children's re-
sourcefulness that I had intended. But the book has continual repercussions. Apart from inspiring (so the authors
told me) similar books in Japan and in Spain, and apart
from translations, it was the basis for a course in 1999 at
the Department of Social Anthropology at the University
of Manchester. I was invited, with the film-maker Mike
Dibb, to talk to members of the course, and to return after
six months to view their work.

The people there reminded me sharply of changes
in urban childhood since my book was compiled (even
though I had pointed to the erosion of the child's freedom in the city by urban redevelopment for the benefit
of property speculators and for the out-of-town motor-
ist). One student had searched the streets of Manchester
for the sight of children and found that, apart from in-
fants in prams, there was not a child to be seen. Another
project suggested that favorite places for children, other
than shopping centres, were the *interior* environments
of home. It was hard for the researchers not to conclude
that the child of the new century is an *indoor* child. In
the British climate better heating *enlarges* usable indoor
space, just as increased private motoring *diminishes* outdoor space.

My original book had a chapter on "The Girl in the
Background" observing that boys experienced, explored,

and exploited the environment far more than girls. But one group in the project compared the capacity to make use of the central shopping district by putting video equipment into the hand of groups of thirteen to fourteen year-old girls and boys. The result showed a notable lack of cohesion among the boys and far greater competence both in reaching agreement as a group, and in exploiting the usefulness of the environment, among the girls. These two findings are a reminder that urban childhood has changed since I compiled that book. But the experience was also a reassurance that books, once launched, become a point of reference and can take on a life of their own. Don't you too find that a book, thanks to the existence of public libraries as well as specialist bookshops, has a continuing potential circulation?

*I think that, nowadays at least, this is much more a matter of readers recommending a title or lending their copy to others. I regret to say, as one who was greatly dependent on his local library as a boy, that public libraries seem to have entered a terminal decline. And small independent bookshops are being squeezed out by, on the one hand, the large multiple booksellers in cities and big towns, and Internet buying on the other. The latter threatens in turn second-hand booksellers, who are increasingly closing their shops and operating exclusively "on line." What specialist bookshops are you thinking of? The Freedom Press Bookshop for one, I guess. And the Intermediate Technology Bookshop in London, which you praise in* Reflected in Water. *And a significant number of others?*

No, I am bound to agree that the number of others has diminished. When I travelled around the country for lecturing engagements, until about ten years ago I knew of alternative bookshops in many British cities, and know that few of them still exist.

I am not so pessimistic as you are about the public libraries, which, like you, I have used from childhood. If you can forecast your needs, the local public libraries in Britain will obtain virtually anything you can reasonably expect through Inter-Library Loans and the British Library Lending Department. However, statistics for book-purchases by both public and university libraries show a continued decline.

*I feel certain that you, as a non-computer-user yourself, have in no way faced up to the extraordinary electronic revolution of the last two decades. Some anarchists are very excited by it. And I certainly see many positive features. But overall I'm alarmed by the eagerness with which people are prepared to enslave themselves to the new technology, having no regard for the terrible mistakes of the first Industrial Revolution, and also by the collapse of face-to-face interaction which it entails. Do you have any thoughts on what is almost certainly the most important change of our times?*

For me the most important communications revolution has been the universal availability of the photocopying machine! When friends laugh at the way I cling to a portable manual typewriter, I point to the fact that my output of words is greater than theirs. My reasons for not adapting myself to the newest revolution in communications are because I am both old and poor, and have different priorities. Our grandchildren seem to be computer-literate from birth. If I were an anarchist editor today I would rejoice in the availability of the global anarchist press on the Internet and especially the fact that on the "A" website (http://www.anarca-bolo.ch/a-revista) I can read a detailed presentation in English of every issue of the *Revista-A* from February 2000. From the point of view of anarchist journalism, this kind of facility, spread around the world, seems to me exactly what I needed forty or fifty years ago.

*I think we need to discuss the significance and impact of the events of 11 September. You will recall that, when you originally mentioned this topic for our conversations, I brusquely dismissed it as of only temporary significance. As well as being fatigued by the constant media attention, I was reacting strongly to the contention that the world had permanently altered as a result of the attacks.*

*But the war in Afghanistan and the Bush administration's switch from its expected isolationism to a U.S. global intervention on a scale never before experienced in peacetime, as well as the ongoing controversies which have erupted between uncritical supporters of American foreign policy and its opponents, have proved me to have been at least partly wrong.*

*If I could believe that as a consequence of 11 September public awareness in the USA about world affairs and their country's destructive input to them had been transformed, I would be delighted. But instead Americans, unable to understand that internationally they are loathed as much as they are loved, seem to have identified themselves as the "good guys" and their opponents, of whatever stripe, as "bad guys."*

*In contrast, I consider that the USA "had it coming" since it has been, in effect, at war for the past fifty years with the peoples of Latin America, Asia, and Africa. Unlike most other nations, it has not suffered civilian casualties and domestic destruction since the Civil War, way back in the 1860s; yet U.S. administrations and American capitalism have committed terrible crimes and have been responsible for tens of thousands of deaths, indeed probably hundreds of thousands.*

*Despite this I have to say that, in spite of their "evil empire," I do like many, or even most, Americans very much, especially for their personal warmth and democratic straightforwardness. I lived and worked in the States for a year and I found that an enjoyable and enriching experience. Contact with the ever hard-done-by Black Americans was particularly rewarding. Yet I was disturbed by the sheer ignorance and overwhelming parochialism of the average American.*

I can remember how, at the end of the Second World War, and after the atomic bombs on Hiroshima and Nagasaki, there was discussion in anarchist and pacifist circles about the way that nuclear weapons, delivered from a distance by aeroplanes, had made resistance to tyranny impossible. Orwell took this view, and Alex Comfort expressed a different opinion in his pamphlet *Peace and Disobedience*, which impressed me greatly in 1946 and which you reprinted in your collection of Comfort's political writings.[5]

He argued that

> . . . it is an essential feature of the new ways of war that they are indiscriminate, and can be used only against a community . . . The very states which are able to make and use atomic weapons are singularly vulnerable, by their very complexity, to the attacks of individual disobedience . . . The contentions of anarchism have been strengthened, not weakened, by the advent of new weapons.

5    Alex Comfort, *Against Power and Death*, edited by David Goodway (London: Freedom Press, 1994).

And Comfort went on to claim that "Megalopolitan government is utterly irresponsible, it displays an irrevocable tendency to war, and its cities are increasingly indefensible."

In the half-century and more since Comfort was writing, we can read his comments as an anticipation of the kind of guerrilla activity that has characterised struggles against European and American imperialism, but, with hindsight, we can read the particular sentence I have just quoted, as a forecast of events like the attack on the twin towers of the World Trade Center on 11 September 2001. For during those fifty years the governments of the United States have imposed their will around the world, installing local rulers acceptable to American export markets, and using its global air power to inflict devastating loss of life among defenseless civilians. Discussing this issue in 1994, the English playwright Harold Pinter drew attention to the U.S. bombing of Laos, Cambodia, and Iraq, its intervention in the Dominican Republic, Granada, and Panama, and to the deaths of hundreds of thousands of people in Indonesia, Guatemala, Nicaragua, Chile, El Salvador, Angola, the Philippines, Turkey, Haiti, and East Timor.

He added that "The dirty work is normally done by the locals, of course, but the money, the resources, the equipment (of all kinds), the advice, the information, the *moral support*, as it were, has come from successive U.S. Administrations."[6]

By comparison, the dirty work of the attack on the twin towers required the willingness of a few young men to throw away their lives, with no equipment apart from a few simple weapons to terrify plane crews, but with

---

6    Harold Pinter: letter to the *New York Review of Books*, June 9, 1994.

careful training in aircraft management and, presumably, map-reading. To me this is abhorrent because, just as I support the right to live of all the victims of American foreign policy, I support the right to live of those plane passengers, and would have wished a more useful life for the young men who terrorized their last minutes. The dreadful truth is that more Americans make no connection at all between this sensational, lethal, and isolated incident and the foreign policies they have failed to reject for decades.

Harriet visited lifelong friends in the U.S. last summer, and came back with exactly the same misgivings as yours about the "overwhelming parochialism" of American understanding of events. Ordinary citizens failed to understand the impact of their country's foreign policy, and are bewildered by the hatred that is engendered by it. Neither the anarchists nor any other minority group has found a way to widen from minority audiences, in spite of exciting local experiments in radical radio and, more recently, widespread direct access to the Internet.

Probably most of your friends in the U.S., just like most of mine, have belonged to that faithful minority who have spent lifetimes opposing both the overseas and internal policies of governments of both major U.S. parties. Was it their ultimate influence on American opinion, or was it the growing level of U.S. military casualties, that finally brought the U.S. withdrawal from Vietnam?

Contemporary Islamic militancy is an American creation. Arundhati Roy explained this in the minority American press:

> In 1979, after the Soviet invasion of Afghanistan,
> the CIA and Pakistan's ISI (Inter Services
> Intelligence) launched the largest covert operation

in the history of the CIA. Their purpose was to harness the energy of Afghan resistance to the Soviets and expand it into a holy war, an Islamic *jihad*, which would turn Muslim countries within the Soviet Union against the communist regime and eventually destabilise it. Over the years, through the ISI, the CIA funded and recruited almost 100,000 radical *mojahedin* from 40 Islamic countries as soldiers for America's proxy war. The rank and file of the *mojahedin* were unaware that their *jihad* was actually being fought on behalf of Uncle Sam. (The irony is that America was equally unaware that it was financing a future war against itself.) In 1989, after being bloodied by 10 years of relentless conflict, the Russians withdrew, leaving behind a civilisation reduced to rubble.[7]

*Yes, I've much admired Arundhati Roy's recent writings on these matters (as well as her activism in India itself). I had hoped that, at the very least, the attacks of 11 September would lead to the USA insisting on the Israelis showing greater respect for the lives and liberties of the Palestinians. But the easy defeat of the Taliban regime and the supine attitude of almost all the governments have allowed, most recently, the bloody military occupation of West Bank towns, whereby the state of Israel—even Israeli society—has lost whatever moral superiority that remained to it.*

*One was already aware of a marked growth of vehement anti-Semitism among Muslims everywhere because of Israel's conduct towards their fellow religionists. I have heard over the years that the notorious 19th-century*

---

7    Arundhati Roy, ("The Algebra of Infinite Justice," *Peacework,* Cambridge MA, USA), November 2001.

*forgery,* The Protocols of the Elders of Zion, *circulates in the Islamic world. This I saw for myself in Malaysia in August 2001. In the bookshop at the tiny airport of Kuala Teregganu, capital of the small, but oil-rich, state of Teregganu, which forms with Kelantan, the Muslim traditionalist North-East of the country, there was on sale the* Protocols *in a glossy South African edition (including also Henry Ford's* The International Jew*). I was tempted, from sheer curiosity, to purchase it—but refrained. It was available, I would add, at a very devout Islamic bookstall.*

I have noticed that even anarchists can fall into the error of assuming that people agree with the governments in whose territories they live, or with political factions associated with their ethnic origins.

Most of these errors are part of the deadly legacy of European imperialism, like so many of the territorial disputes in Africa, or in Indonesia, or in the disputes between India and Pakistan. On Britain's doorstep the gangster feuds between "Catholics" and "Protestants" are part of the same inheritance. For example, I have friends who are "Protestants" from Northern Ireland who believe that they should be citizens of the Irish Republic, and I know others whose origins are "Catholic" who are not interested in a united Ireland. And, like you, I have many friends born in either part of Ireland for whom nationality is irrelevant in their lives.

It is the same with Israel. Obviously we gravitate towards friendships with like-minded people, but I should say that every Israeli friend of mine is a supporter of the rights of the Palestinians, sometimes at personal risk. I am old enough to have had friends brought up in the kibbutz community in the days of the British Mandate, and who sought a joint solution with the Palestinian Arabs.

They, in their old age, are as bewildered as I am that a nation state founded by socialist atheists should have its laws formulated by a religious minority, not only in matters of legislation concerning birth, marriage, divorce, and burial but indeed in the definition of who is a Jew and thus has the right of citizenship.

This is as tragic for Israel as is the rise to power of Muslim fundamentalism in other nations of the Near and Middle East, including those with centuries of harmony and interchange between communities whose nominal religion was Jewish, Christian, or Muslim.

It is now eighty years since Martin Buber warned his fellow Zionists that, if the Jews in Palestine did not live *with* the Arabs as well as *next* to them, they would find themselves living in enmity to them. An Israeli friend of mine, Akiva Orr, was asked about the changes he discerned, returning after twenty-six years abroad. He replied that "The first change I noticed when I discussed politics in Israel is that humanism (the principle that all human beings, whatever the differences between them, must be treated as equals), which was an assumption taken for granted by most Israelis up to 1967, is now upheld by only a minority." And he added that "A second, immediately noticeable change is the sharp shift towards religion . . ."

*This was bad news for everyone, but especially for anarchists.*

Yes, it was. Precisely because of the subsequent worship of the nation-state it is important to remind our readers that many of the *kibbutzniks* were atheist socialists, had no interest in nationalism, and wanted nothing more than to live at peace with their neighbors. I remember the father of my old friend Gabriel Epstein saying to me sorrowfully, "We already had a hundred nation states. Isn't it a joke to have a hundred-and-first?" Somehow, since those days, history has been rewritten, and we have been persuaded that traditional Judaism demanded the re-occupation of Palestine, and was somehow sanctified. Anarchists, including Israeli anarchists, reject this opinion.

*Yes, I was very struck when editing* Against Power and Death *to find Alex Comfort writing in 1948 in a journal called* New Israel*: "Why am I uneasy about a Jewish State? Because I am uneasy about any state. I am never ready to support uncritically the birth of a new authority . . . The Jewish people have shown themselves uniquely capable of living together in a non-coercive, defensible, social society. If their unique pattern is replaced by the orthodox pattern of government, ministries, parliaments, presidents and prisons, the future of free institutions far outside the circle of Jewry will be at risk." I had thought that this was Alex being typically original. I hadn't appreciated that others, including Jews themselves, had argued the same at the time.*
    *Do you see religion as the opiate of the people?*

No. It is more of a stimulant than an opiate. Exactly like nationalism it stimulates hostility and aggression towards others. Plenty of observers have noticed that people who are kind and considerate towards others in their personal life can become mass-murderers under the banner of God and the State.
    The early anarchists, and the socialist movement in general, assumed that we would all outgrow God and ethnocentrism, but it has not happened. I read recently about a tract entitled *Traité des trois imposteurs: Moise,*

*Jésus, Mahomet*, "written by a pseudo-Spinoza, first published in Rotterdam in 1712, and often burned or banned
ever since." What would be the effect of such a polemic
written today? You and I would be entertained, but believ-
ers in any of those three prophets would feel strengthened
in their faith, threatened by the evidence of unbelief and
hostility to belief.

In Britain the ancient laws against blasphemy still
exist. They were continually challenged by our mutual
and much-missed friend Nicolas Walter (1934–2000)
who wrote a history of *Blasphemy Ancient and Modern*
(London: Rationalist Press Association, 1990). The blasphemy laws were concerned, of course, only with the
Christian religion; and in 2001 the British government at-
tempted to extend the blasphemy law to cover all religions
in a new crime of incitement to religious hatred. This
was vigorously opposed by my trade union, the Society of
Authors, and other organisations, and was withdrawn.

*A far greater proportion of Americans are Christian
church-goers than of, say, British or Italian or French people, while U.S. administrations and American capitalism
have committed terrible crimes around the globe. And thus
we return to that appalling yet, at the same time, alluring
society on the other side of the Atlantic.*

*As for American informal imperialism and the irre-
sistible force of American cultural imperialism all over
the globe, Europe not excluded, what can be done to resist
them? Don't get me wrong. I love American music, above
all jazz and the Blues and its classical tradition, as well as
American literature.*

I'm in exactly the same situation as you. First of all in that
my most-loved American friends like David Koven and

Audrey Goodfriend are veterans of the anarchist press there, or like Taylor Stoehr, the editor of Paul Goodman, belong to the same anarchist subculture as me, as are the publishers of our conversations. Secondly, because my favorite novel, for a lifetime, has been *Huckleberry Finn* and another of my most cherished books has been Thoreau's *Walden*. I am in no position to criticize American cultural imperialism as I have to accept that the global language is English, even though I would argue that it should be Spanish, which is far more mellifluous and, unlike the absurdities of English, has a logical spelling. Like plenty of the revivers of traditional jazz in Britain, for example Humphrey Lyttelton or the anarchist George Melly, I fell in love with New Orleans music and the Blues through minority records, actually sold as the Parlophone or Brunswick "Race" series (meaning Black) when I was fourteen in 1938, and when that year the veteran broadcaster Alistair Cooke presented an unforgettable radio series on the BBC called (in Whitman's phrase) "I Hear America Singing." I have been in love with American music ever since then.

Your American dilemma has existed ever since Alexis de Tocqueville completed his reflections on *Democracy in America* in 1840. Beneath the surface of so much that seemed so admirable, and indeed astonishing, in the evolution of the social and political institutions of the young United States, de Tocqueville observed a tendency towards conformity which he deplored. "Every citizen," he wrote, "being assimilated to all the rest, is lost in the crowd, and nothing stands conspicuous but the great and imposing image of the people at large." He concluded, just as you conclude today, that "I know of no country in which there is so little independence of mind and real freedom of discussion as in America."

But if we look back today at those writers whom we would now regard as 19th-century America's pre-eminent contribution to world literature, two things are clear. First, it is evident that as individuals they were an absolute contradiction of de Tocqueville's generalization. Each of them displays a quite staggering independence of mind. Secondly it is also evident that any one of them would have echoed his opinion. I am thinking of Thoreau, Hawthorne, Melville, Whitman, and Mark Twain. Whitman was always singing the praise of American democracy, but his vision was of a democracy of autonomous individuals. He said it was "a great word whose history, I suppose, remains unwritten, because that history has yet to be enacted." And Mark Twain, despite his enormous worldly success and popularity, bitterly concluded that the only commandment that Adam would never be able to disobey was, "Be weak, be water, be characterless, be cheaply persuadable." In order to become his own man, let alone to become a virtuous man, the hero of Mark Twain's great masterpiece had to break loose from American civilisation. The saving grace of the United States is that in each generation it produces its own profoundest critics.

*By American cultural imperialism I am not thinking so much of the ever-increasing dominance of the English language—important and worrying though that is—but rather of Hollywood's ousting of indigenous cinemas, of McDonald's and Kentucky Fried Chicken fast-food outlets appearing in towns throughout the world—even in Kuala Teregganu, where they would have to use halal meat (and were certainly catering for locals, not tourists)—and American popular music and American dress having unlimited appeal for the youthful in whatever society.*

I know exactly what you mean. Every parent in Europe knows the grotesque price of trainers probably made by child labour in the East. Our youngest, Ben, won a course in jazz at a celebrated music college in New Jersey. When he moved from the airport to the bus station at Newark, another young man waiting for the bus pointed to his shoes and said, "You don't survive in *this* state with those on your feet."

Neither of us have any idea about how to change the culture of the young. In Britain, plenty of people have stood outside McDonald's handing out leaflets describing the legal case that has become known as McLibel. Two anarchists, Helen Steel and Dave Morris, were sued for libel by the McDonald's Corporation in 1990

> for the distribution of London Greenpeace leaflets criticising McDonald's, the food industry and multi-nationals in general for promoting unhealthy food, damaging the environment, monopolising resources, exploiting workers, targeting and exploiting children and causing animal suffering.

McDonald's sued the two anarchists for libel and the case resulted in the longest trial in English history. It began in June 1994 and lasted for 314 days in court. McDonald's spent an estimated £10 million on prosecuting these two anarchists. They were awarded £60,000 in damages and the Appeal Court reduced it by £20,000. In the anarchist journal *The Raven* (no. 43, [2002]) Dave Morris and Helen Steel wrote:

> Two days after the verdict, in a Victory Celebration Day called by the McLibel Support Campaign, over 400,000 anti-McDonald's leaflets were defiantly

distributed outside the majority of their UK stores, and there were solidarity protests around the world. We were elated. As experienced campaigners we knew throughout that what really counted was the court of public opinion, the determination of activists to refuse to be silenced and to ensure that an oppressive law could be made unworkable by co-ordinated mass defiance. That is what happened in this case.

One thing about which we know little is whether the famous McLibel case in Britain had any effect at all on the young customers of McDonald's.

*Let's return to music. I believe music is the most important of the arts for you. I know that your sons Barney, Tom, and Ben are all musicians. And didn't you once write an article advocating that "every school day should begin with singing and dancing"?*

What you say is true. But if you ask why I enjoy music most of all, it is perhaps the fact that I am not obliged to write about it. For years if I read a book or saw a play (including important performances from the 1950s onward like the London visit of the Berliner Ensemble, or later excitements like Peter Weiss's *Marat/Sade* play, or the British performances of Dario Fo's plays) it was in order to make intelligent anarchist comments. Music has always been free of this obligation.

My own musical education had nothing to do with school, but had everything to do with the BBC which reached 80 percent of British households by the beginning of the Second World War. In Britain there is a habit of sneering at the elitism of the BBC in prewar days, a criticism which is not shared by people who were children in the 1920s and 1930s. Jonathan Rose, the author of a very interesting piece of historical research, *The Intellectual Life of the British Working Classes* (New Haven: Yale University Press, 2001), reports how the BBC as a musical educator "was lavishly praised in the memoirs of all sorts and conditions of working people." I myself was privileged. At the famous Promenade Concerts at the Queen's Hall in the 1930s, I went, firstly with my parents and later with my older brother, to hear all the new legendary soloists of that era.

Many decades later, I became by chance the guardian of two boys who attended Wandsworth Comprehensive School in South London, which had a famous choir whose teacher, Russell Burgess, used to maintain that "every child can sing." Sadly, when he died, the celebrated choir died too. He made no impression on the boys I was looking after, but one of them, inspired by the enthusiasm of a language teacher, became a global authority on the Blues.

Later still, another London Comprehensive, Pimlico School, made the bold decision to have a special course for Young Musicians, and when Barney and Tom left their local primary school they attended it. We rejoiced in the incredibly rich musical experiences they enjoyed. Our youngest, Ben, was a primary school pupil in the city and a secondary school pupil in the country, with no special attention to music, but still moved on to earn a university degree as a performer.

They all impress me by their *versatility*, in picking up an instrument and playing every kind of music. And I notice that their appreciation of a whole series of works in the repertoire, from Bach to Britten, has a greater validity than mine, simply because they, having performed in them, know them from the inside.

Thanks to the BBC as a musical educator, I was aware that Britten was the bright young composer whose development was worth watching, and I thought that, just as it was a privilege for Beethoven's contemporaries in Vienna to watch his work over the years, up to the final great quartets, so we would spend a lifetime in expectation of some new triumph from Britten. In some respects this was a justified anticipation of his output, despite the "brooding, obsessive nature of much of Britten's later music," as his biographer Humphrey Carpenter put it. I remember that, when Britten died in 1976, Vernon Richards wrote to me, remarking that his *Serenade for Tenor, Horn and Strings* was the finest musical masterpiece of the 20th century, and that the Britten/Pears partnership was the century's most productive marriage.

I was quoting Yehudi Menuhin when I wrote that "Every school day, anywhere in the world, should begin with dancing and singing," and I went on to describe the educational philosophy of the 19th-century French utopian Charles Fourier. In his ideal community, Harmony, the primary years of education would be shaped around cooking and opera, these being activities which develop every kind of human art or skill and do not rely on book-learning. They are also fun. I was writing at a time when the devastating simplicities of the Thatcher government were blaming the loss of Britain's export market on the education system which was under attack for wasting time on the arts instead of training exporters. As I explained:

> It's a joke really, since if we value schools by the currency-earning potential of their students, the art colleges have earned this country far more millions for the export economy through their steady output of rock musicians who despise the

officially-approved values, than any amount of thoroughly-trained industrial designers could possibly bring it.

But you will know, as the editor of Herbert Read, that his book *Education through Art*, published in 1943, was a key text for teachers, not for what it said, but for the ideal it promoted. You quoted in the introduction to your collection *Herbert Read: A One-Man Manifesto and Other Writings* (London: Freedom Press, 1994) his own observation that "It is not often realised how deeply anarchist in its orientation . . . *Education through Art* is and was intended to be. It is of course humiliating to have to confess that its success (and it is by far the most influential book I have written) has been in spite of this fact . . ."

The book appeared with, as George Woodcock put it, a "formidable battery of psychological, anthropological and pedagogical authorities" and, as Read admitted, was "too difficult for the people it might most benefit." Paradoxically, this did not matter. He had given intellectual respectability to those teachers who know how vital the creative arts are in a child's development. A month after Read's book appeared, an advertisement in a weekly paper invited people to attend a meeting in London to discuss the formation of a Society for Education through Art. It exists to this day.

*This leads us into the large topic of education. I would argue that the central social process is how we socialize and inform the next generation, i.e., the process of education. From the 1940s through to the 1970s educational developments seemed so promising, as features of the libertarian experiments of the early 20th century were applied throughout the system of public education. But now we have been returned to a pedagogic Stone Age. Do you despair? Or do you—you are usually able to in other fields—see any signs of hope?*

Britain, like many countries, has several concurrent education systems. For the rich, paying fees for their children's schooling there are "preparatory schools" operating up to the age of thirteen and the so-called "public schools" for that age upwards. For the rest of the population, paying for schools in national and local taxation, there are primary schools and secondary schools. These are referred to as "state schools," although they have been operated, since 1870, not by the state but by local authorities. There is also a tiny network of "progressive schools" of which the most durable is Summerhill School. In addition, some parents exercise their right to educate their children at home.

I agree with you that the incoming Thatcher government of 1979 introduced a pedagogic prehistory. It introduced a National Curriculum, specifying for the first time in British educational history, precisely what was to be taught in schools, and it deluged teachers with forms to fill, certifying what they and their students had done. It invented "league tables" which indicated that certain schools performed well (in middle-class Anglo-Saxon areas) and that other schools performed badly (in districts with low income, high unemployment, and with the children of recent immigrants from all over the world). The collapse of the British manufacturing economy was attributed, hilariously, to the "half-baked progressive ideology" allegedly taught in the teachers' colleges in the 1960s.

I have several reasons for not despairing. The first is that I know that the people who pour scorn on teachers would be utterly lost if faced by a class of fifteen-year-old rejecters of the education machine. They have never faced the fact that we live in a profoundly anti-educational culture, and they have no idea about how to win the young.

The second is that teachers, faced with the task of winning the young to the value and the values of education, are automatically subversive. It is often this fact that wins the sympathy of the class. Most of us have met people who were children in Hitler's Germany or Stalin's Russia, and who remember with affection those teachers who, subtly but continually, separated themselves from the regime and thus won the confidence of their students.

Teachers from other countries, hoping to learn from British schools, would not dream of approaching the government's department of education. They enquire from organisations like Human Scale Education, Unit 8, Fairseat Farm, Chew Stoke, Bristol BS40 8XF.

*This has been a sad period for you. During our conversations not only have we lost Vernon Richards, Michael Young, and your old employer and friend, the architect Peter Shepheard, but now a fourth friend of yours has died: the brilliantly innovative, Argentine-born scientist, César Milstein.*

You are right. When I was asked to join the Freedom Group in 1947 I was its youngest member, so today I am the sole survivor from those days. What remains sad is the death of friends like Marie Louise, before they had the pleasures of growing older, as well as the opportunity to make the contribution to anarchist ideas that they were uniquely capable of making.

César Milstein, described at the time of his death in March 2002 as "one of the best-loved and most important scientists of the 20th century," was, like his wife Celia, a biochemist, who won a global reputation as "the father of monoclonal antibodies," and was awarded a Nobel Prize in 1984 and a host of other awards. My friendship with the Milsteins was a result of the links formed by the global anarchist press many years ago. In the 1950s they frequently translated my column from *Freedom* for the celebrated anarchist journal *La Protesta*, while César's father, Lázaro Milstein, would make a further translation for *Dos Fraye Vort*.

The Milsteins first came to Cambridge in 1958 and returned in 1963 (permanently as it transpired) after one of a series of military coups in Argentina. One of my happiest memories of them from those years was when they took me to a concert by the Cambridge University Madrigal Society, with the singers on punts, lit by Chinese lanterns, on the river, singing English madrigals of about the year 1600. Celia and César remembered singing the same works years before at the University of Buenos Aires. I was enchanted by the fact that the English madrigal composers—people like Dowland, Weelkes, and Wilbye—were as transatlantic in appeal as the European anarchists.

César's father had emigrated from Ukraine to Argentina at the age of about fourteen, knowing not a word of Spanish, and went to a Jewish farm colony in the interior where he learned to read and write through the reading and discussion of books like Kropotkin's *The Conquest of Bread*.

*Milstein was a biochemist who moved sideways into immunology. I have for long been fascinated by the fact that such anarchist intellectuals as there are have tended not to be the lawyers, economists, and historians, so prominent in other socialist movements. Rather anarchism has received disproportionate contributions from intellectuals active in the life sciences, geography, the arts, and the like.*

*Paul Goodman puts it very well in a piece you once sent me: "Kropotkin was a geographer and agronomist. Reclus was a geographer, Fanelli an architect, Pelloutier a lawyer specializing in labour and civil liberties cases, Malatesta had studied medicine, Morris was an arts-and-craftsman, Ferrer was a progressive educator. These humanistic and, so to speak, ecological vocations are very different from being an economist, politician-lawyer, academic, or technologist."*

I can certainly think of a dozen anarchist friends of yours and mine who fit Goodman's categories. Think of biologists like Harold Sculthorpe or graphic artists like Donald Rooum and Clifford Harper. Or think of the people I was fortunate enough to meet in the architectural world. I have mentioned Walter Segal, a refugee from Nazi Germany who worked in obscurity in Britain for years until he devised a simple, yet subtle technique of house-building that enabled very poor people to house themselves. I think too of Giancarlo De Carlo, who when he came to London to receive the gold medal for architecture, mentioned his first meeting with the anarchists in 1945, "exceptional people who have been the most important encounters of my life."

*Goodman continued in the passage I've quoted (it's from his review of James Joll,* The Anarchists, *in* Peace News, *12 February 1965): "An analogous point has often been made . . . about the anarchist labor-unions as opposed to the Marxist or individual-craft unions. The anarchist unions are either exquisitely skilled, like the watchmakers or printers, or spring up in dangerous or self-reliant occupations like seafaring, lumbering, mining, farming. Both these groups believe that they can cope very well without*